Science and Faith

Books by Eric Gans

The Discovery of Illusion: Flaubert's Early Works, 1835-37. University of California Press, 1971.

Un Pari contre l'histoire: les premières nouvelles de Mérimée (Mosaïque). Paris: Minard, 1972.

Musset et le drame tragique. Paris: Librairie José Corti, 1974.

Le Paradoxe de Phèdre suivi du "Paradoxe constitutif du roman." Paris: Nizet, 1975.

Essais d'esthétique paradoxale. Paris: Editions Gallimard, 1977.

The Origin of Language: A Formal Theory of Representation. University of California Press, 1981.

The End of Culture. University of California Press, 1985.

"Madame Bovary": The End of Romance. Boston: G. K. Hall (Twayne's Masterwork Studies), 1989.

Science and Faith

The Anthropology of Revelation

Eric Gans

Rowman & Littlefield Publishers, Inc.

ROWMAN & LITTLEFIELD PUBLISHERS, INC.

Published in the United States of America
by Rowman & Littlefield Publishers, Inc.
8705 Bollman Place, Savage, Maryland 20763

Copyright © 1990 by Rowman & Littlefield Publishers, Inc.

All rights reserved. No part of this publication may
be reproduced, stored in a retrieval system, or transmitted
in any form or by any means, electronic, mechanical,
photocopying, recording, or otherwise, without the prior
permission of the publisher.

British Cataloging in Publication Information Available

Library of Congress Cataloging-in-Publication Data

Gans, Eric Lawrence, 1941-
   Science and faith : the anthropology of Revelation / Eric Gans.
      p. cm.
   Includes bibliographical references and index.
   1. Philosophical anthropology.   2. Language—Origin.
3. Revelation.   4. Religion.   5. Culture—Origin.
6. Anthropology—Philosophy.   7. Religion and science—1946-
I. Title.

BD450.G317   1990   215—dc20   90-42472 CIP
ISBN 0-8476-7659-5 (alk. paper)

5 4 3 2 1

Printed in the United States of America

∞™ The paper used in this publication meets the minimum requirements of American National Standard for Information Sciences—Permanence of Paper for Printed Library Materials, ANSI Z39.48-1984.

Table of Contents

	Preface	vii
1.	The Scene of Origin	1
2.	Revelation and Its Object	21
3.	The Mosaic Revelation	49
4.	The Christian Revelation	85
5.	Conclusion: Science and Faith	117
	Bibliography	125
	Index	127

Preface

THE RECENT OFFENSIVE of "creation science" against the teaching of the theory of evolution has generally been dismissed in academic circles as a side-effect of the conservative trend of the Reagan era. But although "creation science" in itself is of little intellectual interest, its emergence reveals a fundamental point of conflict between science and religion that is of more than topical significance. This conflict concerns the origin and nature of man. In contrast to the embarrassing attempts of religion to muddy the waters of the natural sciences, the debate between science and religion on the subject of human origins is a true *dialogue de sourds:* neither side is capable of assimilating even the most fundamental contributions of the other.

The premise of the present work is that generative anthropology, which hypothesizes that the origin of man and human language took place in a founding event, provides the basis for a fruitful dialogue between human science and religion on this crucial point. It has become our habit to look on primitive religion as a source of tribal man's understanding of nature, and civilized religion as an expression of moral values, but to consider in neither case the real cognitive strength of religion, which is to be found in its comprehension of the human condition.

Science and Faith is a demonstration of the power of generative anthropology to extract from religious texts clearly formulated and in principle "falsifiable" anthropological theses. It is my hope that this work will help to persuade the reader that the paradigm defined by the originary hypothesis constitutes a new stage in the progression of human science toward a unified vision of man.

Passages from Martin Buber's *Moses* are reproduced with the permission of HUMANITIES PRESS INTERNATIONAL, INC., Atlantic Highlands, NJ.

1
The Scene of Origin

RELIGIOUS FAITH has by now made its peace with natural science. Spirit no longer attempts to lay down the law to matter, even to living matter. Yet it would be a mistake to see this peace as a defeat for religion. Willingly or not, the intellectual force of religion has in fact been strengthened by this strategic retreat from territories that could no longer be defended against the inexorable advance of the physical and biological sciences.

For the "human" or anthropological sciences still have a fundamental lesson to learn from religious thought. The abstractions of *homo economicus* and *homo sociologicus* must be grounded in a species-specific concept of man that religion, however imperfectly, provides, but that the positive science of anthropology has preferred to ignore. This situation will change only when the human sciences abandon their dream of emulating the natural sciences by studying the human as just another "objective" domain of empirical investigation. Anthropological science can only assimilate the human truth preserved by religious faith if it succeeds in creating a plausible *hypothesis of origin* for a human consciousness distinguished from its animal counterparts by its ability to use representations. Appearances to the contrary, a generative hypothesis is equally necessary whether one considers human consciousness to be "computable" or whether one views it as the emanation of a soul created by God. Yet it cannot be denied that this necessity has been more clearly grasped by the holders of the latter position than by the defenders of the former. In order to become a truly fundamental science of man, anthropology must absorb the lessons of religion, and this requires that it demonstrate a far greater concern and respect for the form and content of religious experience than is presently the case.

The common presupposition that the origin of human consciousness was gradual and therefore unconscious is an attempt to avoid dealing with the problem of man's uniqueness with respect to his animal ancestors. No doubt man's upright posture, "neoteny," and cerebral cortex development are the products of an evolutionary process lasting several hundred millennia and ending only some 30,000 to 40,000 years ago, when our species attained more or less its present physical form. But what is concealed by paleontological discoveries is that "man" is undefinable by physical measurements, including those made on his brain. Man must be defined by his *mind*. Whether we call this defining element "soul," "consciousness," "internal scene of representation," or even "language-acquisition device," the real debate on this point is not between science and religion, but between generative anthropology, which takes as its basis the punctual origin of man, and positive anthropology, which conscientiously studies the various aspects of proto-human evolution but cannot formulate a hypothesis to explain how man the user of language emerged from it.

The origin of man can be approached only through a hypothesis that, unlike those of the natural sciences, cannot be verified empirically. The scene of origin is the model of an event that left no physical traces, although its mental traces are coextensive with the human cultural universe. The scientific detachment we can exercise with regard to this scene, which allows us to propose a possible causality for it, is the product of the subsequent evolution of the human mind, without which science would be inconceivable. But the undoubted heuristic superiority of the scientific method over religious intuition in extra-human matters does not imply that the founding event, with its before and after, should be dissolved into an indefinitely extended causal series in which "events" have only a statistical significance. Human science has no justification for ignoring the universal religious intuition that the origin of the human mind cannot have been gradual. Only once it was already in possession of its representational means could the mind experience more or less continual periods of expansion. Its birth cannot have gone unperceived, for what was born was precisely a new modality of perception. The mind that does not yet know itself is not yet a mind; what is initially played out on man's internal scene of representation is the first act of representation itself. This act must designate something, but it is not enough that its designatum become an object for consciousness; the representing act must remain associated with it. Nor can this be a Pavlovian "association" between two worldly phenomena like the appearance of food and the sound of a bell. The association between the representative signifier and its signified must preserve the *intentionality* of its use in the originary scene, as preserved in the memory of the individual participants in the scene. The other signs of human language are generated by analogy with this originary model.

The first human event must have appeared to its participants as a *revelation*. The first object the presence of which seemed unusual enough to be *re-presented* must have entirely overturned proto-man's sense of regularity, of "causality." We still experience today distant vibrations of this overturning. Only by becoming attentive to these vibrations will we be able plausibly to reconstruct the event that was their source.

That there exists a scene of origin for human representation, that is, a scene of the origin of language, is a fundamental thesis independent of the specifics of any particular reconstruction of this scene. Hence the hypothesis of origin to be presented here, one adapted from my previous work, *The End of Culture*,[1] makes no claim to be definitive. It has been constructed according to the primordial rule of scientific discourse that requires the *minimality of the hypothesis,* a rule often formulated in terms of "Ockham's razor"—that mental entities should not be multiplied beyond necessity. I have assumed that the origin of representation must be an event and that the originary event must be a *scene* retained in the memory of its participants for the following reasons:

1. The scene must be *collective* because language, like all forms of representation, is a phenomenon of human communities rather than isolated individuals. The convention that associates the signifier with the signified cannot be created by a "social contract"; it must be realized *in*

actu in such a way that the mental signified associated by all with the signifying act has its origin in the same material referent.

2. The individual member of the proto-human collectivity is still an animal and can therefore only be moved by appetites. The systems of "ritual" constraints employed by higher animals to assure collective order all involve hierarchical dominance. But if in this scene proto-man undergoes the fundamental change that starts him on the road to hominization, this can only be because the animal mechanisms that are part of his genetic heritage have proved insufficient to maintain order at the critical moment. The cultural transmission of information is not the product of an *élan vital* driving evolution to the development of ever higher life-forms; it emerges at the moment when the old genetic system of transmission ceases to be effective. At a certain point in the evolution of animal intelligence, the lability of appetite in a collective situation becomes too strong to be controllable by hereditary mechanisms. Greater intelligence means a greater ability to imitate the actions of others, and this ability puts an increasing pressure on the mechanisms that must constrain such imitation where it interferes with the governing order of the group. At the critical moment, the survival of the group requires that a new mechanism be found.

The process of hominization after the originary event will be dependent on genetic selection. But the scene can affect selection only indirectly; its influence is dependent on the fact that, within the scene itself, genetically determined mechanisms of communication are suspended in favor of the new mechanism of representation that has emerged from the interaction of its participants.

3. The "arbitrary" sign that is the origin of language must have its source in appetitive behavior. The acts associated with animal rites are incapable of bearing a designative or referential meaning; their significance remains immanent in them and cannot therefore become representational. The gestures of domination/submission that characterize the relationship among wolves or chimpanzees are, as the originary sign will be hypothesized to be, aborted appetitive gestures (*e.g.*, sexual

"presentation"), but these gestures merely express, or *incarnate,* domination or submission. In contrast, in the originary event, the aborted gesture of appropriation transforms the renouncement of its object into a *designation* of this object.

These considerations bear on the minimality of the hypothetical scene.[2] This minimality has a necessarily provisional character; as with any construction that claims to be scientific, a more minimal hypothesis can always in principle be conceived.[3] I have here distinguished between the primary sequence of events, which alone is essential to the (minimal) hypothesis, and a number of secondary elements, shown within parentheses, that are destined to give it a plausible foundation in the lives of its participants:

A group of pre-humans (following a hunting expedition) surround an object that strongly excites their appetite (a large edible animal that has just succumbed to their blows). Everyone is preparing to move toward the object. But each, noticing the appropriative movement of the others (intimidated by the scene's potential for violent conflict), aborts his gesture. This aborted gesture, directed toward the central object, and consequently reinforcing the attention that all already bestow on it, functions as an ostensive *designation* of it. For as soon as everyone notices that, for a certain time at least, no one will seek to appropriate the object, each understands the others' gesture as "meaning" the object. The scene will remain in their memory as centered on an object that so excites their appetite that it paradoxically becomes for that very reason untouchable. The aborted gesture of the individuals on the periphery, which is prolonged in the kinetic imagination of each toward the object, becomes the *sign* of the object. The reproduction of this sign not only evokes the object but *designates* it to the other participants of the scene. This gesture is thus the first act of representation, and its collective performance constitutes the originary group as a *human community* bound together by its common observation of the ethical constraint realized in the substitution of the gesture/sign for the act of appropriation.

SCIENCE AND FAITH: THE ANTHROPOLOGY OF REVELATION

* * *

Each religious faith claims to be definitive and universal, yet its truths, unlike those of science, are rooted in the particular, in a revelation fixed in space and time. Lacking this, faith is nothing but "deism," a pantheism founded on the daily revelation of cosmic order, religiosity rather than religion. The hypothetical scene of the origin of language is a primordial model of revelation with respect to which the founding events of particular religions stand as historical sequels. The originary scene constitutes the fundamental revelation prerequisite to all higher religious experience, which it consequently allows us to understand in an entirely new light.

In biological evolution each fundamental transformation takes place only once. The branches of the genealogical tree of species do not converge. (Indeed, the same applies to all levels of being; atoms and their constituents can only be identical from one end of the universe to the other because they have a common source—as the currently accepted "big bang" cosmology presupposes.) Man's qualitative as well as quantitative distance from other species implies that the biological rule of unique genesis must apply to him even more rigorously. If our hypothesis truly describes the birth of man, the founding event it postulates must have occurred only once. Human monogenesis can only occur at the extreme limit of biological monogenesis: its concentration in a unique event.

Biological speciation does not take place as an event; it requires a unique *population,* not a unique community. Although it is thought today that new species evolve through a relatively speedy and local process (in opposition to Darwin's idea that species were slowly transformed *in toto* into new ones), the selection of a new genotype is only possible over several generations. But the genesis of the human species is not reducible to the general model of biological speciation. Man is defined by his possession of systems of representation that permit him to transmit to other members of his species large quantities of context-sensitive information that could not be borne by the slow and limited process of genetic mutation and transmission. Non-human species have no scene of origin; specific experiences may modify or "condition" their behavior, but can effect no irreversible change in their relation to the objects of their appetite. Man is the only animal for whom collectively remembered scenes, or events, exist. The hypothetical event involves no immediate biological modification, but it promotes such modification by revising the selection criteria within the proto-human species to include the supplementary aptitude for survival bestowed by the discovery/invention of language.

In proposing the originary hypothesis and defending its plausibility, one cannot ignore positive social science's fundamental resistance to man's origin in an event—to precisely what religious intuition grasps, and until now has been alone capable of grasping. The new anthropology proposed here holds forth the hope of a *rapprochement* between the discourses of religion and science. But for such a convergence to be conceivable, the opposition of these two discourses can no longer be accepted *a priori;* it must be seen as a barrier to be overcome.

The originary scene is not a "myth of origin." To the positive mind, any explanation that presents itself to the imagination in the form of a scene is suspected of being mythical. The term "myth" is a pejorative label that has been applied to scenic discourses since the Presocratics. The label easily sticks to narratives that explain natural phenomena in cultural terms, that present old figures as new knowledge. In human matters, the question of its appropriateness becomes much more delicate.[4] To avoid all danger, positive science is ready to label as myth any scenic explanation whatever, even when the phenomenon that needs to be explained is nothing other than the scene of representation itself.

Positivism is not a simple excess of zeal, a flawed method. Its mistrust of the scene is a reflection of the power of the scene. This power was formerly exercised by religious institutions that only reluctantly softened their hostility to empirical science after many battles and sacrifices. It may still appear the highest goal of science to pursue the fight to the finish now that the weight of institutional authority is preponderantly on its side. But the power of the imaginary scene has not disappeared; it has only been displaced. The advancement of human science requires us to reject the positivist illusion that "demythification" can dissipate once and for all the danger of unscientific arbitrariness emanating from the imaginary scene. In reality, positivism only condemns certain uses of the scene as mythical in order better to be able to take refuge in others the scenic nature of which it refuses to acknowledge.

For positive anthropology is not without explanatory scenes of its own. In discussions of the discovery of fire, of the fabrication of tools, even of the origin of man's upright posture, "scenarios" abound. What feature of these scenes makes them acceptable without reservation to scientists who reject as mythical any hypothetical scene of origin?

Here is a "hominid," a kind of ape in the process of becoming a man without it being possible to designate the exact moment of the transformation. Such a figure appears to pose no problem to anthropologists, although its doubtful position between beast and man makes it suspiciously akin to the half-human half-animal divinities of primitive religions.

But let us continue. Our hominid enters a forest with a group of his fellows. He perceives a leopard hidden in the leaves of a tree, ready to attack; he lets out a cry and points to the predator. All flee. End of scene.

This scene will have served in anthropological discourse to explain the origin of language. And how have we, the readers, been touched by the explanation? We have put ourselves in the place of the hominid who discovers the leopard, we have felt the same danger, and at that moment we have *understood* that, in his place, it would be entirely natural for us to do the same thing as he did. "In his place," even if he is not quite a man, for what is easier than to shout when one has vocal cords, or to point when one has fingers...? But this kind of explanation through scenic identification is the defining operation of mythical discourse. This "positive" scene is in fact a myth. The being whose performance generates the explanation is not a man like ourselves, because his acts would then require no explanation whatever. That we are nevertheless expected to explain these acts by putting ourselves in his place implies that nothing is in fact demonstrated in this scene, that its operation is merely tautological.

In contrast, the hypothetical originary scene presented here, in explaining the passage of the not-yet-human to man, explicitly excludes any specifically human element from the motivation of its actors. If its plausibility requires that we put ourselves in the place of its participants, it equally requires that we make the effort to identify with beings that do not yet possess either the apparatus of signification or that of desire (in contrast with simple appetite). This hypothesis is at the very least a myth of a newly reflective and demanding sort, whereas our "anthropological" scene exemplifies myth's most pernicious trait: the intellectual *comfort* inherent in the unexamined assimilation of cultural acts to the responses of a "second nature."

Why is the positive anthropologist so ready to believe in the truly mythical scene, while reserving his condemnation for the other? Could it be because the originary scene is *not sufficiently* mythical?

For there are scenes and scenes. The comfort of the anthropological scene betrays more than mere intellectual laziness. Within the scene there is fear and trembling, but for those who contemplate it from without, there is no danger. Nothing is truly *revealed*. Our imaginary experience is circular: either the hominid is already a user of signs, hence already a man, or his gesture is not a sign, and is therefore unable to serve as an explanation of the origin of language. One might wish to affirm that the gesture is not performed as a sign, but that it *becomes* a sign during its manifestation and/or interpretation. The scene would then become truly originary. But as soon as we dare to present this scene, even without modifying a single detail, as the model of a *unique and irreversible event,* the positivist recoils before what he perceives as a betrayal of his intention. For his scene was merely "illustrative." Such scenes do not *decide* between beast and man. They are situated within a million-year-long transitional period during which the hominid remains an indefinite mediating species, near enough to man for us to understand its acts, yet far enough for this understanding to count as an explanation.

In order for this anthropological myth to function, the separation between man and not-man cannot be defined; the in-between must extend before as well as after the scene, and, finally, *nothing must occur.* Positive anthropology can welcome the scene of myth with open arms so long as nothing happens on it. The non-event appears to foil the sinister power of the "myth of origin" while allowing us to shift comfortably from intuitive identification with the actors to causal demonstration. What is new here in comparison with traditional myth is that the shifting takes place not as an event on the imaginary scene, but entirely within our perception of it, that is, on our own imaginary scene of representation that is tacitly assumed to be a place wholly secure and "private." Without anything having occurred, the hominid transforms himself into man. One of the most important transformations in the history of our planet, not to say the universe, occurs in a mere change of attitude that never *takes place* on the scene, but for which the scene serves as a pretext. We fix the frontier between the human and the almost-human at some arbitrary point, and then show that everything that exists on one side must have "always already" existed on the other. The aim of the non-event is to convert the frontier into a non-frontier, to demonstrate the *toujours-déjà*. Positive thought and Derridean deconstruction commune in the ritual murder of the originary event.

The function of any hypothesis of the origin of man, including those that are traditionally called myths, is not to transform into a fictitious event something that was necessarily a gradual process, but, on the contrary, to present a plausible reconstruction of what *must have* occurred as an event. But Western anthropological science, which classifies and interprets the myths of every society in the world, is insensitive to their significance as originary hypotheses. The anthropologist does not fear these "ethnological" myths; he manipulates them with perfect ease, for it is child's play for him to transform mythical events into non-events, or "structures." What he rejects is the scene of the genesis of man, which in our society is associated not so much with primitive myth as with our own Judeo-Christian religious tradition.

The by now familiar assimilation of the Bible to mythology should not permit us to forget that human science was not born among the Tikopia or the Trobrianders, but in Western Christian societies, with the Jewish minority—Marx, Freud, Durkheim, Lévi-Strauss—playing a disproportionately significant role. It is our own religious tradition that most intimately incorporates scenic genesis into its vision of humanity. The revelations made to Abraham, to Moses, to the prophets; the great moments of Christian history, from the Annunciation to the apparition on the road to Damascus, are the elements of a progressive history of transcendental revelation. Although the Bible contains retrospective fabrications and adaptations of Middle-Eastern myths, its most significant events must be considered as historical, not only when they agree with archaeological data or contemporary testimony, but when they describe revelatory experiences that could not have been simply invented. These experiences are the core of the unique historicity of the biblical religions. The anti-historicism of the human sciences—including much of the history written today—was born in opposition to this religious historicity.

The roots of contemporary positive anthropology do not lie in militant atheism; on the contrary, the atheism of Feuerbach, Marx, and Engels remains faithful, in its fashion, to the historical dynamism of progressive revelation. These roots are rather to be found in that "religiosity" so characteristic of thinkers of the nineteenth century who hoped to find in primitive societies the lost fullness of their experience of the sacred.

Myths relate events, but their kernel of experiential truth is often difficult to grasp. Anthropologists prefer to find in the fabulous and fantastic aspect of myths a proof that they do nothing but recombine the elements of the sole events that positive science recognizes: the endlessly repeated occurrences, changing only over centuries, of everyday life.

Ethnology and its interpretative techniques were born in an attempt to transcend what appeared to its founders as the ethnocentric narrowness of biblical historicity. The search for the kind of myth from which events can be excluded is the product of a revolt against the tyrannical historicity of the Bible by the well-thinking Protestants—Frazer, Tylor, Robertson Smith—who were the founders of ethnological science.

The privileged form of primitive religion is the rite, the weakened event, deprived of its originary uniqueness, frozen in a repetition ever less comprehensive and less alive. The Bible was thus first explained through ritual, before being read in the twentieth century as a concatenation of "mythemes" from which the slightest relation to real events is a priori excluded. Although early ethnology did not deliberately oppose religious revelation, it was the product of minds who had lost contact with the revelatory content of the texts they had considered canonical.

Why should this incomprehension be generated ineluctably by the very tradition that gives the event the greatest role? All fabulous embroidery aside, Christ on his cross is a historical event, not a myth. It is not that we have gradually forgotten what such an event signifies: it is that we have forgotten that this signification can only be understood in the context of a particular event. Biblical history has come to appear "ethnocentric"; biblical revelation, from an experienced reality—which the object of faith must always be—has become the referent of a merely intellectual *belief* that differs merely by a yes or a no from non-belief.

But it is counterproductive to deplore the forgetfulness into which these revelatory events have fallen. Bemoaning our lack of spirituality is a dangerous substitute for the necessary effort to promote human self-understanding by means appropriate to our era. In defending the anthropological value of the spiritual discoveries of past times, we must avoid the opposite error of condemning modernity as the locus of a new fall of man. If the spiritual life of past ages could have sufficed for our own, that life would not have been extinguished. The great prophetic spirits whose words some borrow to scourge the modern era were well aware that the revelations that nourish men and allow them to progress must one day lose their potency. The resistance to revelation is a constant theme of the Old Testament, and even more so of the New; but new revelations of human truth, more rational and *by that very fact* more spiritual, are always necessary. We should not expect those of our era to come from traditional religions, and even less from the secular or ultra-religious cults that sometimes substitute for them. They are more likely to emerge from within an anthropology that is able to construct a hypothesis of man's origin without depending on either religious fideism or positivist agnosticism.

In permitting us to rediscover the revelatory nature of human genesis, the originary hypothesis does not simply pick up the thread of sacred history that was lost during the nineteenth century as the climax of a secularization process that goes back to the Renaissance and beyond. The anthropological truth of the central biblical texts of revelation can only be understood today in the context of a theory of the revelatory scene that avoids recourse to supernatural beings or forces.

The supernatural is the name of everything that poses a problem in matters of religion, of everything that hinders modern man from understanding the cognitive content of revelation. By the same token, the refusal of events betrays a fear of the transcendental that seems to intrude whenever an event is made a bearer of significance. In the presence of the event to its participants, we sense a shadow of the divine presence. The positive spirit condemns the concept of an originary scene as mythical because it suspects in the central figure a disguised divinity to whom we would alienate, like the participants themselves, the human truth revealed in the scene. This suspicion is a product not of the study of myths but of the Judeo-Christian tradition itself, the limits of which are revealed by the incomprehension of its own modern heirs.

The biblical text is the fruit of a revelatory experience without equal that has played a central role in the domination exercised today by Western culture—in forms varying from economic liberalism to Marxism—over very nearly the entire globe. Because this text refers to a supernatural being, it is all too simple either to attribute it to the efforts of cynical priests or exalted visionaries, or, conversely, to make of its genesis a mystery that it would be indecent to seek to penetrate. But reverence and disparagement alike offer inadequate readings grounded on inadequate anthropologies. The more ostensibly modern of these attitudes is only the inverse reflection of the other; both agree that the biblical writings are incomprehensible unless a supernatural ingredient is added to the human experience they describe. It is in fact of little importance whether we assume that the transcendental divinity who gives this experience its revelatory import was hallucinated or invented after the fact, or whether we claim that he was indeed present in person. At least the last interpretation admits more humbly than the others its inability to reduce the content of a new revelation to the recombination of preexisting elements.

The originary hypothesis is an attempt to understand the birth of the transcendental domain of representation. The desired object is translated into the "other world" of the sign; what significant memory preserves is not the formal relationship between the signifier and its signified, but the imaginary prolongation of the sign toward its referent. The real collective scene makes possible the imaginary individual scene by isolating its referent in the center and thereby transforming it into an object of desiring contemplation. To really possess the object would be nothing; but because it is desired as unattainable, its possession becomes the model of a satisfaction without common measure with the satisfactions of this world. It is this impossible imaginary satisfaction that consecrates the object in the founding event; the central referent is the bearer of a collective peace, of a *deferral*[5] in whose contemplation the nascent human community can commune.

The originary scene is only conceivable as centered on a real object. But its centripetal constitution is ambiguous. For the center is on the one hand the object surrounded by the circle of participants, yet on the other, it is a mere locus determined geometrically from the circumference. The central object is "overdetermined" as both object and center. This originary ambiguity eventually results in the separation of the abstract scene of logical thought from the concrete revelatory event. The classical form of this separation is the opposition between science and religion that the present work attempts to transcend.

The aporia is not one of causality—the eternal question of the chicken and the egg—but of what we might call transcendental ontology. Both the appetitive object and the proto-human group are requisite components of the originary scene. But the object does not exist solely for man; its being is independent of the scene. Thus while the independent being is consecrated by men as the very being of the scene, the scene itself, once constituted, is capable of reconstituting itself around other objects. Viewed from without, it is the human circle, not the divine central object, that is the *sine qua non* of humanity. The object existed before, will no doubt exist again, whereas the circle is a new creation. Whether the central place be filled by a buffalo or by a rhinoceros, or by a proto-human of the same or of another species, should therefore be for us a secondary matter. But in thus subordinating the object to the geometrical locus, we risk forgetting the eventful nature of the scene on which this central locus was first consecrated and on which the transformations in our understanding that we call revelations have always taken place. It is this willful forgetting of the event that has led anthropologists to propose eventless "scenes" in the place of generative explanations.

The fundamental anthropological structure, that of *significance,* from which alone *signification,* the use of signs, can be understood, is the human circle turned toward its central locus. But the disillusioned wisdom that is expressed in Mallarmé's phrase *rien n'aura eu lieu que le lieu* (nothing will have taken place but the place) too easily sets aside the being that occupies this place and that alone defines it as such for its first worshippers. The locus *per se* is an abstraction; the place never exists without an occupant. It is easy enough to denounce the vanity of the desire that elects first one object, then another, while its focus always remains the same. It is the center itself we desire, it is said, never really the being that occupies it. We desire with the desire of others; we join the circle that surrounds the least trifle, while the central truth remains transcendental. But this truth itself could only reach human consciousness through the mechanism of the scene. Trivial as our worldly desires may be, they are generated by the same process that produced the great moral revelations of history. We may conceive of a pure locus, an empty center, but we can never experience it; nothing will ever be revealed to us there.

The double nature of the scenic center explains the inadequacy of any ahistorical anthropology, be it conceptual or "empirical." One central being reveals its contingency only in comparison to another. The freer centrality of the second demonstrates the arbitrary nature of the first, initially in the act and later in the words we attribute to the central being in the form of a person-god.[6] Man's historicity depends on the uniqueness of the originary event. If every language shares the same principles, if everywhere we find more or less similar rites, it can only be because all human societies share at least the inception of their history. Man has been able to invent techniques and forms of social organization because he possesses an apparatus of representation that defers the appetitive act while exposing the desired object to contemplation. The scene of representation, once created, becomes "portable"; the sign extends its communal function to realize between two men, or between a man and himself, a *virtual community* mediated ultimately by the original scene.

The persistence of virtual community, of language and all that goes with it, does not reduce human history to a powder of non-events. Whatever happens on the scene of representation is an event, and the historical greatness of an event cannot always be measured by the number of its participants. All individual revelations, the successors of the original collective revelation, communicate through the scene we share as a common heritage. But we should not seek in rituals, which more or less directly imitate the configuration of this scene, the sources of new revelations. Ritual is the opposite of revelation. Nothing new must occur there; the only evolution the rite undergoes is the gradual draining away of the truth it was its task to preserve. Rites die and are replaced by others, keepers of new revelations. But these revelations themselves never occur within the framework of ritual; their privileged locus is the individual imagination, whose intuitions are tested only after the fact by the community.

NOTES

1.   Berkeley: University of California Press, 1985.

2.   The question of the minimality of the originary hypothesis has been treated more extensively in *The End of Culture*. The substance of the argument is as follows: For the originary scene to effect a durable transformation, its consequences must involve a material advantage for its participants. This advantage comes about through the non-violent sharing and consumption of the central object after the delay or "deferral" in the process of appropriation brought about by the signifying gesture. In the present context, we are less concerned with the material conditions of preservation or reinforcement of the originary gesture than with its spiritual consequences.

3.   In the anthropological domain, a process of progressive minimalization must be substituted for that, formalized by Karl Popper, of "falsification" followed by formulation of a stricter and consequently more easily falsifiable hypothesis. Truly specific anthropological hypotheses, as opposed to those concerned only with the worldly reality that man shares with other natural beings, are not generally falsifiable by new data because they aim at the *comprehension* and not the simple physical determination of the data in question. Ultimately the notion of "scientific method" as it is practiced in the natural sciences depends on the transcendental status of the human subject with respect to his subject matter, a relation that evidently cannot obtain when man attempts to understand himself.

4.   The analogue in the human domain is a discourse that purports to explain anthropological phenomena in cultural terms, that is, that expresses an "ethnocentric" ideology. But in order to expose such myths, a reductive Voltairean rationalism does not suffice; the specific ethics of different societies can only be evaluated in the context of a general anthropology.

5.   *Deferral* is the translation of *différance,* a neologism coined by Jacques Derrida. It uses the double meaning of the French verb *différer* (both "differ" and "defer") to express the non-co-presence of the different significations that Saussure had seen as opposing each other in an atemporal structure. It is an emblem of Derrida's critique of structuralism; to differ is to defer a decision between two alternatives. But Derrida gives no anthropological basis for this notion, which he at the same time insists is not a traditional philosophical "concept." Generative anthropology conceives the notion of *différance* more concretely; the central function of the creation of signification in the originary

event is the deferral of conflict among the members of the nascent human community. The differential signification of the central object defers conflict by deferring/differentiating the incompatible drives toward its assimilation.

6.   The "opening of the center" is the main theme of Eric Voegelin's great study of religion and culture, *Order and History,* 4 vols. (Baton Rouge: Louisiana State University Press, 1956-74).

2
Revelation and Its Object

WHAT IS REVEALED by revelation? Can its meaning be reduced to propositional knowledge? How otherwise can we speak of its truth? And if revelation contains a human truth, why is this truth presented as the communication of a supernatural being?

The traditional religious and scientific answers to these questions offer only the choice between fideism on the one hand and positivism on the other. Our sole chance to find more satisfactory answers is to deepen our understanding of the originary moment in which the human capacity for representation emerges from the union of the universal scene and the particular event.

The positive spirit, accepting without acknowledgement the gift of the original event, constructs a placeless metaphysical abstraction of the scene on which it generates models of all aspects of the natural world. The religious spirit accepts the gift with such gratitude that it permanently fixes in the center of the scene an originary being to whom its thanks can continue to be addressed. Either the scene of representation descends "supernaturally" from above or it evolves "naturally" from below; neither positive science nor religion is willing to regard it as of merely human origin. But if we hope to understand man on his own terms, to create an anthropology that is neither transcendental nor reductive, we must hold fast to the hypothetical originary event as the source of both the constraining truth of revelation and the experimental freedom of natural science.

The more extreme varieties of positivism like Skinnerian behaviorism or sociobiology deny the specificity of the human. These views are influential today because they help reduce the uncomfortable and inexplicable gap that separates man from other species. The traditional positivist position, however, is that of an agnostic humanism that turns away from the "undecidable" debate over origins to proclaim representation a tool of man, the rational animal. In this view, even if the historical concreteness of the original event were granted *ex hypothesi*, it would be a mere contingency; the center of the scene is no more than the fixed focal point of the attention of the periphery, like the stage of a microscope. There is in principle no difficulty in understanding or evaluating the products of revelation; one need only bypass the contingent peculiarities of the sacred center and calculate the usefulness of the informational content to its human beneficiaries on the periphery.

This attitude found its original spokesmen in the fifth-century Sophists, for whom man as "the measure of all things" could invest his significance wherever he pleased. The Sophists were rhetoricians who taught their pupils to exploit the revelatory capacity of communal language for private ends. Since language makes things appear, there is no need for the appearance it evokes to correspond with reality. Hence the Sophists were accused of teaching men to empty the scene of all prior meanings in order that the worse cause could be displayed on it as the better. In the two and one half millennia since the Sophists, the ethical pretensions of humanism have not been given a firmer basis. Humanism still affirms that "man" is the measure of all things; but "man" exists only in communities linked by the historical contingencies that the ritual centers of religion commemorate. Generative anthropology has no reason to disagree with Michel Foucault's celebrated dictum that the humanist abstraction of "man"—although not the idea of "man" as such—is no longer a functional anthropological concept.

If the objects appearing on the scene of representation were indeed "things" and not man himself, the Sophists would be right and revelation would have no specific function. All historical revelations are ethical: they concern not the natural order, but the order of the human community. It is because ethical truth, unlike propositional truth, is dependent on the particularity of the scene of representation that it historically appeared in the form of revelation. This does not require us to accept uncritically the old mystery of a transcendental divinity who imperiously manifests himself to man. Yet no interpretation of the anthropological truth of a revelation can abstract from its revelatory origin.

In the originary hypothesis, the sacred center-as-being appears to the participants as the cause of the event and of the scene insofar as it preserves the memory of the event. The aborted gesture as sign is addressed to the center, but at the same time it is the center that reveals to the participants the meaning of their gesture. The inaccessible center and the men of the periphery communicate by means of a revelatory dialogue that is the foundation of the "linking" we call *religio* or religion.

One can only be struck by the inadequacy of the nineteenth-century attempts to counteract the anguish of the retreat of the sacred by providing "natural" explanations of the origin of religion. It was claimed not only that the Judeo-Christian tradition could be explained by primitive rites, but that these rites in turn derived from sentiments inspired in primitive man by a host of natural phenomena: disasters or regularities, the power of the sun, death and decomposition, and so on. Although such explanations were considered quite reasonable in their day and are treated with considerable respect even now, they stand in fact at the zero degree of anthropological epistemology. Like the scenarios of the origin of language discussed in the preceding chapter, they never raise the question of the origin of the "natural" sentiments they attribute to their proto-human subjects. Because we can identify with these sentiments, they can be projected onto creatures whose evolution into human beings like us is precisely the point at issue. These theories reflect a pre-Darwinian conception of man as a being placed on earth in more or less his present physical state but lacking in those cultural traits, like religion, that distinguish him from the rest of the animal kingdom, traits that this cultureless "man" must then proceed to invent. Not that modern anthropological science has found more convincing explanations of the origin of religion; as the old theories have fallen into discredit, it has simply preferred to shift its field of inquiry—and its eventless myths—to less obviously dangerous terrain.

The fundamental subject-matter of religious revelation is not the mysteries of nature, with which the pre-human being could never have concerned himself, but the mystery of the human community that the scene unites around its center. Each participant sees all hands reaching toward the desired center; each finds himself in the position of one against all and hesitates to prolong his gesture. The gesture continues to be imaginarily directed toward the object, but since it cannot be completed, it proposes its referent to universal contemplation, as each imitates and is aware of the gestures of the others. Unlike the aborted or diminished acts of animal rites of submission, this sign does not merely communicate the renunciation of its object; it *refers to* it. The center is the indispensable mediator of communal communication; it distinguishes and distances each of the participants both from itself and from his neighbors. The relative isolation of each participant is determined by an equilibrium between the centripetal attraction of desire and the centrifugal repulsion that holds him at a distance. This distance reveals men to each other as at once the same and different—the same with respect to the center, but different through the specificity of each *in his place.* The equilibrium of the scene of representation thus brings into existence the human community as the differentiated order of the individuals on its periphery.

The members understand that they form a community through their designation of the center in a gesture both communal and individual. This designation institutes among these desiring beings a peace based on mutual comprehension. In order for the gesture to be a truly signifying, a truly *linguistic* act, each must be convinced, must *have faith,* that his neighbor's gesture has the same meaning as his own.

What is thus revealed through the center of the scene is the new form of non-violent communication that it mediates, no longer founded on the mechanisms of dominance and submission that maintain order in animal societies. The participants can only create a new order through the mediation of the sign if they remain in perfect equality with respect to it. There are no doubt some in the group who are stronger than others, but the centrifugal power of the center is such that even the strongest does not dare to move toward it in the face of the manifest desire of all his fellows. The communal order is established for the duration of the scene as the order of beings formally equal by virtue of their possession of the minimal criterion of humanity: equality before the scene of representation. This fundamental principle of moral equality is not "egalitarianism" in the modern sense, for there are as yet no rights to distribute, no ideal of social justice at which to aim. It is limited to the universal obligation to respect the interdiction imposed by the sacred center by signifying rather than appropriating it. These characteristics are established once and for all as man's *sine qua non,* the foundation of the human order instituted in the scene.

This minimal equality—which by no means abolishes the remaining inequalities of animal life—is the fundamental ethical truth, the foundation of what Kant would call "practical reason." For the first men, no necessity antecedent to the event itself imposed on them the truth of their new human status; only through their experience of the event was this truth revealed to them. Revelation implies a teleology, an intuitive conviction that the new path it has opened must be taken. The revelatory experience is irreversible; the community will always bear the imprint of this moment. Each event of revelation is part of a cumulative history. What has once been revealed will remain so, as long as man's collective memory endures. This is the only real guarantee of historical "progress," even if human lives do not necessarily improve either physically or morally from century to century. That after a revelation things can go badly, even worse than before, is no counter-argument to this thesis; some truths are harder to bear than others, and sometimes the means to bear them are slow to develop.

Propositional thought gives the answer to an already asked question, but revelation displays the question and the answer all at once. What is revealed in the originary event is the organization of the collectivity as a peaceful community on the scene of representation. This revelation emanates from the center and its ethical content is realized *in actu* each time that men reconstitute the scene around a new center—each time, in fact, that they use language.

We may draw from this examination of our hypothetical scene of origin a few conclusions that will help us to understand the great historical revelations. Revelation does not occur *sub specie aeternitatis* and does not concern the more or less immutable order of nature. It is historic and human, historic because it is human. It expresses an implicit judgment concerning the path its recipients must follow, but this judgment appears in the form of a conviction imposed by the situation itself. Thus "false" revelations can occur—those whose path, once taken, shows itself to be the wrong track. The falsity of revelations, like their truth, is pragmatic, demonstrated by practice rather than logic. History never exhausts all its possibilities. More or less probable circumstances might have reversed the signs of true and false. Even at the outset; for man might never have come into existence. The teleology of revelation strikes us as tautological because it is the teleology of the victorious. But this provides no basis for the denial of its truth. History cannot await logical certitudes. It is because it is made in action, in the event, that revelation is necessary.

Because the originary hypothesis affirms the orientation of language toward the scenic center, it contains the condition *sine qua non* of its own eventual "revelation." The original content of language is already a hypothesis of the origin of language. But the circle is not closed; the hypothesis implies only the possibility, not the reality, of its own historical formulation. In the realm of practical thought, one cannot avoid regarding the present human world as the *telos* of originary humanity; but anthropological theory must guard against any foreclosure of possibilities that would tend to give history the appearance of a foreordained chronological succession. Not only is the sequence of history not determined from the start, but its periodization always remains subject to revision—by the competing hypotheses of today, but more importantly, by the historical events of the future.

Even if we put aside, "in brackets," as it were, the evidence of history, the very form of representation is that of an event. The word does not gradually emerge from the womb of nature; it is pronounced, and the imaginary scene on which it makes itself heard springs up as if *ex nihilo*. The interlocutors' attention to the words they exchange is fixed on the present instant where something absolutely new is about to appear. This newness of speech reflects the *discrete* and *arbitrary* nature of the linguistic sign, its qualitative difference from all the "signs" of non-human nature.

The arbitrariness of the linguistic sign offers a demonstration in the small of the historical, or, more precisely, the historigenic mechanism of revelation. The word is arbitrary because another would have served just as well; nevertheless, only *this* word is available to refer to *this* thing. It is of little importance whether it be *vache* or *cow;* but it is necessary that the animal be designated by some word or other. If this necessity disappears, the word will fall into disuse, and ultimately be forgotten. For no logical necessity requires that a language possess a name for this animal; it is the verdict of history that causes the word to come into being and to continue to exist. The object of many etiological myths is nothing but an etymology. The appearance of a new word is a minor revelation, dependent on the originary revelation of language itself. In both cases, history must demonstrate the effectiveness and consequently the irreversibility of the new creation. Even if we cannot know the primordial form of the word that became *vacca* in Latin and *vache* in French, we know that its first use was an event. Its ensuing evolutionary history, as peaceful as the animal it designates, in no way disconfirms the hypothesis of its punctual origin; on the contrary, it illustrates an essential aspect of the historical operation of revelation—that it founds an *institutional* duration. Each word is a revelation in miniature, an *ex nihilo* creation, but it is at the same time framed by the primary institution of language and hierarchically subordinate to the primitive revelation that instituted it. All revelation is ethical, and the great revelations are those which irreversibly transform the most fundamental human relations.

We thus begin to observe the anthropological utility of the notion of revelation. We must rid ourselves of the falsely reasonable attitude that regards the process of human self-discovery as an eventless accumulation of knowledge on the model of the evolution of an academic discipline. Man's ability to extract general laws from series of empirical observations depends on a language each word of which bears the marks of its origin in a particular event. Each event is contingent, but it is folly to think that in abstracting from any given contingency we can avoid contingency in general. Historical contingency is necessary, just as in the linguistic system an arbitrary word for *cow* is necessary. The original circle must have formed itself around something, and this something was revealed at that moment not as the arbitrary occasion of this formation, but as the necessary source of a new human order.

The place of revelation always remains the scene of representation, but not necessarily as a collective scene. For once the first scene has been established, all others that derive from it are *virtually* collective. The object that attracts the attention of a single individual will inspire in him the intuition that it would also interest his fellows. The ethical nature of revelation, and the revelatory nature of ethics, are the result of the persistence of the human community united both concretely and virtually around the scene of representation, which is at once communal and individual, real and imaginary.

* * *

Why, once the originary ethic of the human community has been revealed, do new revelations continue to prove necessary? Once the absolute equality of men before the scene has been established, what need have they to change their principles? Does not the primordial ethic contain potentially all ethics? These questions may be reduced to two: (1) Why was the originary ethical truth insufficient to lead man to his present state? and (2) Why must new ethical truths appear again in the form of revelations? These questions address (1) the discontinuity and (2) the transcendentality of ethical truths, which are not secreted gradually by the slow evolution of human behavior, but which impose their necessity in events.

The absolute equality that the founding event established as the fundamental principle of interaction among human beings only obtained with respect to the scene of representation itself; it could not have abolished all at once the system of dominance that presumably regulated the interactions of our animal ancestors much as it does today those of the great apes. But the human ethic was more powerful than the pre-human, and by the time *homo sapiens* appeared we must assume that it had driven it out. The myths of primitive peoples inform us about the extension of the formal equality of the originary scene to the totality of social activity. The primitive equalitarianism that resulted endured down to the neolithic revolution—the beginnings of sedentary agriculture—of only some ten thousand years before the present. Because probably well over nine tenths of human history falls between the first linguistic sign of perhaps several hundred thousand years ago and the rise of hierarchical societies, we may be tempted to view man's more recent history as a fatal hypertrophy of the capacities of the species, analogous to the monstrous canines that brought about the extinction of the saber-tooth tiger. But it is precisely such historical watersheds that revelation determines.

The primitive bands who live essentially by hunting and gathering—and who are often acquainted with the elements of agriculture without being forced by population pressure to make it their chief system of production—do not create permanent hierarchies. The "elementary systems of kinship" that regulate the circulation of women among sub-units of a society or the cycles of ritual precedence of "totemic" clans are equilibrating mechanisms that define individuals within elaborate systems of differences without any of these differences being more central than any other. These systems of circulating differences make primitive society appear strangely like a stable, utopian version of our own "consumer society." This resemblance no doubt explains our unspoken sympathy for its preoccupation with formal differential signs. More importantly, it explains the founding hope of ethnological investigation, that of escaping from the irreversible historicity of Western society to the intellectual paradise of cosmic cycles, of "the eternal return."

There is in the writings of Robertson Smith and especially of Durkheim on primitive religion an understanding of the unity in difference of these societies that is almost ready to spill over into our own. Durkheim the ethnologist finds solutions that Durkheim the sociologist is not quite willing to apply. Does not the system of arbitrary "totemic" differences that functions so harmoniously among the "Aranda"[1] provide a structural model of modern social organization lacking only the market-induced dynamic variability of its elements? But the similarity between primitive and modern society always remained implicit for Durkheim. It emerges only after World War II as the foundation of Lévi-Strauss's structuralism, which hindsight reveals to be the *telos* of the entire ethnological movement. Understanding our own systems of differences according to the model of those of primitive peoples is not mere reductionism. Under its cloak of a respectably skeptical pessimism, structuralism is an act of faith in modern man's ability to recover his equilibrium by renouncing his dangerous discovery of history and relearning the modest wisdom of primitive man, for whom all differences are essential but of the same essentiality. Modern anthropological science no longer wants to hear of founding events or of revelations; it prefers to invest its faith in a form of social organization that appears to be able to do without them.

The highly differentiated equality of the last remaining primitive societies corresponds nonetheless to decadence, or at least to an extreme stagnation. Primitive equality in difference always remains an undifferentiated equality. The advent of hierarchical societies reverses the priority of equality and difference. Today, in the post-modern, post-industrial age, these hierarchies in turn seem to be in the process of dissolving into a host of rapidly circulating and increasingly fine differences; in this society, all are not "equal," but all may be said to be *equally different*. This never-completed process of equalization of difference may stand as the defining condition of modernity.

Because we invest a particular significance in the moral equality of men, equalitarian primitive societies (Rousseau's *société commencée*) appear to us a natural product of man's emergence; in contrast, the hierarchical societies that succeed them seem the effect of a diabolically instigated fall of man. Yet it is more productive to argue that man's original equality provides a basis upon which arbitrarily complex hierarchies of differences can be constructed.

The Western religions that stem from Judaism are founded on a series of historical revelations that no anthropology can afford to leave unexamined. Hebrew monotheism separates itself from the surrounding polytheisms in a far more radical manner than do, for example, Hinduism or Buddhism. The Hebrews, like the Greeks, arose in the margins of the great Near-Eastern empires; but nothing comparable to Judaism ever manifested itself in the East, where China and India built even greater empires on the basis of eight or nine thousand years of agrarian development.

In contrast to this historical uniqueness, the transition from primitive equality to hierarchy is a quasi-universal phenomenon, the first stages of which have been undergone by all but a small minority even among the societies we today call "primitive." The crossing of this demarcation line is a revolution of its own, independent of the technical revolution in food production on which it depends. The fundamental modification of the human order that it initiates no longer derives from a primordial collective revelation, but it is not yet specific enough to originate in an individual revelation or "election," historical traces of which might be preserved in the record. What we must construct is rather an intermediary model, a model of a *secondary revelation*.

Secondary Revelation: The Birth of Hierarchical Society

The origin of hierarchical society is separated from the originary scene by man's entire prehistory. During these millennia, as the first ostensive gesture evolved into the mature linguistic form of the declarative sentence, the human community attained "cultural universality": the incorporation of all the material and spiritual operations of the community into its linguistic vocabulary and their organization into a system of rites and etiological myths. Man's prehistoric ethical evolution was expressed in the stages of the formal evolution of language, from the original gesture through the elementary forms of the ostensive and imperative to the "mature" declarative sentence.[2] For the later, historical moments of ethical evolution, the dialogue of revelation is necessary.

In the purely speculative domain of human origins, hypothetical minimalism is *de rigueur;* but with the birth of hierarchy we find ourselves in the domain of history. And although few anthropological explanations have been proposed for the prehistoric evolution of linguistic forms, there is general agreement on a model of the origin of hierarchical society. The neolithic revolution placed at man's disposal a productive surplus that powerful individuals were eager to acquire for themselves. Hierarchy began, in Rousseau's words, with "le premier qui . . . s'avisa de dire 'Ceci est à moi'" [the first who thought to say, "this is mine"]. But the innovative daring of the first individual who thought to appropriate the surplus by saying "this is mine" must be given a context in which it might have been conceivable. Without at least passive communal acquiescence there could have been no surplus for an individual to appropriate; the community would have insisted upon its consumption on the *potlatch* model of the Indians of the American Northwest.

The birth of hierarchical society was no doubt not a unique event but a development repeated at a number of different times and places; yet no degree of universality can justify our explaining it as an imperceptible, eventless shifting due to unmotivated "technical progress." However many times it may have been repeated under different circumstances, the opening of equalitarian primitive society to the possibility of inequality, like all ethical openings, presupposes the prior intuition/revelation that such an opening was possible.

The End of Culture proposed a model of this transformation that will be briefly summarized here. This model is based on a characteristic phenomenon of certain Melanesian islands described by the anthropologist Marshall Sahlins in his *Stone Age Economics*.[3] These insular societies have undergone a modest degree of agricultural development, but no doubt owing to the absolute limits imposed on expansion (the distances between the islands precluding attempts at political unification) they have remained in a primitive stage of hierarchization that illuminates the path the great ancient societies must have followed.

There emerge in these islands prominent personalities known as "big-men" who, renouncing the relatively easy life of their fellows, undertake arduous supplementary labor in order to accumulate surplus produce. But not only is this surplus never transformed into capital, it is not even consumed by the big-man himself, whose family is often the least well nourished in the village. On the contrary, his efforts at accumulation have as their only goal the honor of presiding periodically over a great feast where his surplus produce will end up in the digestive tracts of a few dozen of his compatriots.

This is at first glance material for a Veblenian satire on "conspicuous consumption," or for an excursion à la Georges Bataille into *consumation* or *dépense*. But the big-man's behavior is neither perverse nor funny. Neither Voltaire nor Sade provide real enlightenment about ritual phenomena. In the sacrificial feast encountered among both primitive hunters and Homeric heroes, we recognize a communal re-creation of the concluding moment of the originary event. Without the peaceful division and distribution of the central appetitive object, the peace bestowed by the aborted gesture would have endured but little, and its memory even less; the survival of the system of representation inaugurated in the originary scene required that it lead to an appetitive satisfaction greater, or at any rate more secure, than that which had previously been available. The divinity in whose name the sacrifice is performed is the transfigured source of primitive revelation in a local form. And the first sacrificial gesture is the designating sign itself, which only became a sign because it resulted from the renouncement of instinctual appetitive satisfaction in deference to the power incarnate in the central figure.

The big-man's celebratory feasts are thus essential moments in the life of the community, and the role of central distributor that he assumes, far from being laughable or sinister, is a temporary usurpation of the functions of the divinity. In the totemic feasts of Australian aborigines where the clan corresponding to the totem plays host to the other clans, the presiding elders occupy a role almost analogous to that of the big-man at his banquet. Almost, but not quite, for these tribes are organized around a principle of symmetry among the clans, each of which presides at such feasts in its turn, just as the prestige of the elders will pass to others who maintain until old age their usefulness to the clan. Such examples illustrate nonetheless the relative *permeability of the ritual center*. As a result of remaining there for a moment before giving up his place to another, a man might acquire, like Eteocles in Thebes, the idea of keeping the center for himself alone.

If this permeability exists previously to the big-man, why take him rather than an Australian clan chief as the first hierarch? The difference is not simply the relative economic superiority of farmers over hunters. Because man is always more of a threat to himself than any natural force, only new ethical conceptions, not new techniques, can motivate transformations of the social order. The big-man does not differ essentially from the clan chief in his accumulation and redistribution of a surplus, for the poorest totemic feast presupposes a surplus, however ephemeral. What specifically distinguishes the big-man is something else: his *individual* and non-prescribed role in the creation of this surplus. Because the big-man's difference does not circulate among the other members of the community as do the pre-scribed differences of primitive society, a permanent disequilibrium emerges between his function as producer/(re)distributor and the role of consumer to which the beneficiaries of his generosity are relegated. In these societies all produce and all consume; but the big-man distinguishes himself from the others in a *ritual* context, that is, at the moment of communal life when the fundamental opposition within the scene of representation between periphery and center is most strongly marked. Certainly the big-man of today has only to imitate the big-man of yesterday to play his role correctly; but the big-man role must be traceable to an origin. It is this origin that is the object of our model of "secondary revelation."

The ritual center is permeable to human activity because after being the locus of revelation it must become a locus of redistribution. The redistributive function anchors the originary revelation within the most crucial domain of practical life, from which it can be extended, with more or less delay, to the others. In any equalitarian social order, it is from the sacred center that the principle of order radiates toward the periphery. This center is not formally empty; it is permanently occupied by the originary central being and its successors, an occupation that spares the members of the community the necessity of making the distinction between the abstract locus "center of the scene" and the revelatory being in the particular place of its revelation.

Human history is driven by the progressive discovery of the liberating potentialities of this distinction for the scenic center: its potential to become the abstract locus of a disinterested metaphysical contemplation, to empty itself of all figures in order to mobilize in a radical community the men of the periphery, or to multiply itself indefinitely through decentralization, permitting each to combine the prerogatives of the center with those of the circumference. These three potentialities of the scene correspond to the three great epochs of Western historical experience, as marked by Greek culture, Hebrew religion, and modern market society. The Greeks discovered the virtues of metaphysical abstraction, the Hebrews the power of the unfigurable God, and modern industrial society, the indefinite potential for expansion inherent in the presence within each individual of an internalized model of the original collective scene.

These far-reaching later developments are all dependent on the original opening to hierarchic society. The symmetric radicalisms of the Hebrews and the Greeks emerge in opposition to, but also on the basis of, the system of archaic hierarchy. The ancient empires, whose cruelty contrasts so strongly with the imagined *douceur de vivre* of the primitive egalitarian order, represent nonetheless a step beyond the latter in the direction of man's great ethical discoveries. From the beginning, every moment of historical progress has been the revelation of a new symmetry between God and Man, the center and the periphery of the scene. The originary event frees the first men from animal dominance-mechanisms by converting the otherness of the appetitive object into a source of absolute power. Man's further liberation occurs through his assimilation of the functions of the sacred center, all of which are subordinate to the single task of keeping the peace among men. One man's assumption of central economic and political power over his fellows, however inhumanly it may often have been carried out, was an essential step in this liberation.

The big-man is able to contribute to the opening of the center because he has discovered the separability of its two essential components, the more radical possibilities of which the Greeks and the Hebrews will later explore: its real-ethical presence as divinity and its imaginary-theoretical operation as abstract locus. This revelation may be expressed more concretely as the *separability of the exchange of representations from the exchange of things*. The big-man understands that so long as the imaginary figure of the central divinity remains intact, he can substitute himself for its material incarnation in the rite and carry out in its place its (re)distributive function. What is changed is not the representation of the divinity but the individual's role in its realization. If in myth it is a god who distributes the fruits of the earth to men, in the concrete act of ritual, men had always to stand in for the god in this function; now an individual dares to *substitute himself* for it.

This substitution in turn will have mythological repercussions. In the archaic kingdoms, the pharaoh or emperor is the eldest son of the gods, and in many respects a god himself. But this mythical transformation is only a reflection of practice; with the big-man and his more powerful successors operating at the center of the scene, the new myths are realized before they are written. Even in the highest cultural accomplishments of the old hierarchical societies, from the Egyptian "novels" to the Babylonian epic of creation, we breathe the dead air of *ideology*. The entire cosmos is depicted as having been conceived and created only to lead up to this monarchy and this monarch, whose authority receives from these texts a broader cultural consecration than that which ritual can provide.

Authoritarian myths always smack of *post factum* justification; but this cannot have been the case at the origin of hierarchical difference. The first big-man cannot have been guided in advance by a myth justifying his usurpation of the center. If such a myth were to exist, he would have had to create it himself. But before dreaming of doing this, he would have had to understand that the center held out to him a possibility of action, of *praxis*. Instead of passively accepting the traditional service of a central divinity understood as the source of the human order surrounding it, an individual can seize the initiative within this order and, in so doing, modify it. Our first hypothetical big-man must have seen the inducement to active participation emerge from the deified center itself. His calling must have been the result of an *election:* a god instructing a man to perform in his name a privileged task. The center reveals to man the possibility, indeed, the duty of occupying it. For it has come to appear, if not empty, then insufficiently full; this is the first stage of "the death of God." As a result of the order created by the originary scene, human society has now become sufficiently peaceful for an individual to discover this essential emptiness and to be inspired by it. His call is not a delusion; its truth is guaranteed by its results. In effect, the community does not react with violence; all sit down at the big-man's table to consume the fruit of his supplementary labor.

This hypothetical event illustrates the movement of revelation in history. The progression of social forms, like that of biological ones, is determined by the attraction of an empty locus to occupy. This locus may lie beyond a geographical frontier; but the form of evolution most characteristic of man takes place within the internal space of the scene of representation. This space, like the pre-modern spatial horizon limited by the "firmament," appears always full. He who senses nonetheless a crack in this apparent plenitude and dares to occupy it demonstrates a more than mundane perspicacity. For the call of the center is not based on sure knowledge; until one has made the attempt, one can never be assured of success. To take a god's place is always a sacrilege; and such sacrilege can only be authorized by this or another god. The old god was a representation of the scenic center, the new or transformed god is another; revelation is a new divine reply to human questions that had previously gone unanswered. The individual must discover this reply as a truth revealed to him alone before daring to test it in dialogue with those who may violently condemn his attempt. Revelation provides its recipient with the certitude without which he would not have the courage to test his new intuition in practice.

This certitude is not merely "psychological," a happy paranoia reinforced by the revelatory hallucination it provokes. To deny the anthropological significance of revelation is equally to deny that of the social order the transformation of which it determines. History becomes a tale told by an idiot where one can no longer distinguish historically significant experience from mental aberration. What may appear "hallucinatory" in revelation is the god who speaks: but the god's voice is the voice of the center from out of which the witness of revelation receives his new answer. For the positive mind, the revealed word is contained in human intuition alone; but the positivist has no explanation for the origin of this intuition. The elsewhere in which the words of revelation originate is the very locus of the origin of language, and the intuition that informs the revelatory experience is that of the identity of this locus with the place of emergence of a new possibility of social action.

What is proposed to the big-man to accomplish is to extend indefinitely the temporary centrality that had always belonged to the givers of ritual feasts. The symmetry of the peripheral human participants with respect to the divine center is not abolished, merely deferred. But this deferral has potentially important material consequences, one of which is a concentration of authority and power that transforms the zealous accumulator of surplus into the recipient of his fellows' tribute, redistribution of which may be more and more indefinitely delayed.

In the big-man's activity, the exchange of representations, in which the essential equality of the originary scene is maintained, no longer dictates an equivalent behavior with respect to the exchange of goods. With the indefinite deferral of this virtual equivalence, which gave equalitarian society its structural stability, material relationships become unequal, and representations are created to justify them. Yet even the ideological burden of these representations is a guarantee of liberation with respect to the previous closure. Now that things and words no longer stand in the symmetrical relation of twin heirs of the originary event, a space has been opened up within which the early forms of rational thought will be able to emerge. For only dynamic thought-forms can provide *post factum* justification for a continuously evolving social order. In contradistinction to the primitive myths that establish a timeless etiology, to be replaced if need be with new myths equally atemporal, the myths of hierarchical societies open out onto history. In order to demonstrate that the present order has been "from the beginning" the *telos* of this history, they progressively historicize the categories of eternity. The most significant moment of this process is the transition from sacred to profane history through the story of the divine creation of man. All men believe themselves the descendants of gods, but now they require the authenticity of this heritage to be continuously reaffirmed from the "beginning" down to the historical epoch within which the present order emerged. The Sumerian king-lists or the Babylonian creation-epic are not products of the stimulation of historical memory by monuments or documents of past reigns. The causal link goes rather in the opposite direction. The historical memory of hierarchical societies is the result of the historicity opened up by the self-centralizing behavior of the big-man, who first found a way to profit from the distinction between the unequal relations of scarce real objects and the equal relations of words.

The self-serving nature of the myths of hierarchical societies should not blind us to the productivity of this distinction between the two exchange-systems. The social order justified by the old myths with all their fantastic detail was in its essence *the order of language itself* as established in the founding event. The equal distance of all from the center was the fundamental condition of the emergence of language, revealed in the symmetry of the designative gestures that allowed them all to be perceived as manifestations of the same sign. The evolution toward cultural universality extended this equalitarian order to all domains of social life, and the myths that justified one or another detail of this extension enlarged at the same time the domain of representation. Yet so long as the primitive equivalence between myth and social practice, guaranteed by the common derivation of both from the originary scene, remained unchallenged, rational thought as the manipulation of words independently of things could not emerge. The arbitrary and fantastic aspect that strikes the reader of primitive myths is not an artifact of ethnocentric prejudice. (How many intellectual sins have been committed in the attempt to avoid "ethnocentric prejudice"!) It is the product of myth's unique explicative operation: the attribution of anthropomorphic desire to the (divine) central figure. The only essential constraint is that myth and social practice both obey the fundamental constraint of the originary revelation: the symmetric equality of all the participants about the center. Mythical freedom is always attributed to the center, not to the human periphery, whose often highly elaborated differences tend toward symmetric equivalence.

What is lost when the center falls into the grasp of the big-man is not a utopian correspondence between myth and social practice, but the more constraining correspondence between this practice and the equality before the scene of representation that is the a priori condition of linguistic communication. The reality of this condition is independent of the generative hypothesis; it is a part of everyday experience. Sociolinguistic differences cannot prevent reciprocal human communication, even among speakers who possess no language in common. But once the big-man arises, material things no longer obey this equalitarian pact. Man's material relationships change irrevocably; all the millennia during which they had remained determined by the equality of the originary scene could create no organic necessity that this equality be perpetuated.

What nonetheless prevents hierarchical society from recreating man in its own image is that its own tendentious use of language can do nothing to abolish the fundamental equality conferred on man by his capacity for linguistic communication. In the face of this equality, the creation of priestly dialects or scripts accessible only to an elite could change nothing fundamental. And equality before the scene of language is also that of the imagination which language always potentially expresses. Hierarchical society can no doubt turn representation to its advantage. But if the exchange of things no longer follows the pattern of the exchange of words, conversely it will never be possible for even the most powerful despot to force the exchange of words to obey the constraints he is able to impose on the exchange of things. The opening realized by the separation of representations and objects will never be closed by either the most seductive mythology or the most overwhelming architecture. This opening, which in the beginning favored the radical inequality of hierarchical society, has always the potential of turning against it.

But the emergence of a form of thought that neither justifies nor depends on the established order cannot await the internal evolution of this order itself. In this opening of the scenic center there must be revealed a word so powerful that all exchanges of things must sooner or later submit to it. It is such a word that was heard by Moses.

Revelation and Resentment

For Nietzsche, the Judeo-Christian religious tradition was the embodiment of resentment, first that of a weak people toward their oppressors (Judaism), then that of the mass toward the elite (Christianity). Nietzsche's reproach is at the same time an expression of involuntary admiration; he well knows that in hearkening to this inadmissible sentiment the partisans of these religions succeeded better in the long run than those who held to the elitist values of the Homeric heroes. The paradoxical success of Christianity never ceased to preoccupy him, and in *The Will to Power*, his unfinished *magnum opus*, he called for a return to the ancient values, a return prepared by the current "decadence" to which, in his view, Christian society has inevitably led.

What Nietzsche grasped with his own resentful genius is the *cultural productivity of resentment*. *The End of Culture* attempted to show that the twin sources of Western culture, the Greek and the Hebrew, have equally as their goal the cultural integration or "sublimation" of resentment. While we may recognize as a partial truth Nietzsche's view of the Hebrew religion, and subsequently the Christian, as products of resentment, we cannot share the illusion under which he granted a privileged status to Greek *arete*. *Menis,* the first word of the *Iliad* and of Western literature, may in effect be translated as "resentment." Achilles' celebrated "rage" or "anger" is in fact his resentment toward Agamemnon who is, in the Achaean army, his hierarchical superior.

There is something intoxicating in the idea that this shameful sentiment that we all share but rarely confess might be the source of our highest cultural creations. In our anonymous night, faintly illuminated by the stars of the mass media whose celebrity seems to incarnate only a superior anonymity, resentment is the only attitude we are certain of possessing in common with the giant figures of the Bible and the *Iliad*. But resentment itself is not the foundation of culture; it is what culture was created to restrain. Religious and aesthetic revelation are society's means for accomplishing the sublimation of resentment. The terrain on which resentment operates is the space opened by the practice of the big-man between the real and the imaginary, things and words. The man of resentment is he who cannot be satisfied to merely think this opposition; the inequality of the two systems of exchange provokes in him a sense of dereliction that only revelation has the power to overcome.

Resentment is a negative revelation, an anti-revelation. A religious moralist might well characterize as "satanic" the temptation to live the resentful experience as though it were complete in itself. We are all familiar with the dereliction of resentment, from within as well as from without. This negative revelation acquires its power from the center of the scene on which it appears, where, instead of seeing a new opening appear, we encounter a closure.

It is not the least demonstration of the power of generative anthropology that it allows us to pin down in a few lines this slippery concept to which Max Scheler devoted a whole book without ever arriving at a definition.[4] Resentment is more than the frustration felt by the first men surrounding the desired object which their desire itself had rendered inaccessible. Here too, no doubt, man finds in the center a closure. But the originary center is only closed with respect to the new capacity for desire that it has itself opened up.

The first big-man discovers in the center a material emptiness that he can fill; like Sisyphus, to whom his periodically annulled and resumed activity makes him curiously similar, we should, in the words of Camus, imagine him happy. But what of his eventual successor? This man needs no personal revelation; the big-man in place is already a sufficient source of light. The incumbent presents himself to his potential rival as a model to emulate; but at the same time he occupies the only place in which the emulation could be carried out. The other, whatever his original intention, finds himself confronted with the scandalous centrality of his generic equal. It is just this sense of scandal at the central other-self that we call resentment.

The central presence of the divinity is experienced as the opening of the scene; that of the human is experienced as its closure. The other's centrality renders the self less free. Yet this very unfreedom is itself an opening. *Pace* Scheler, resentment need not remain confined to impotent frustration. The scandal inspires its own negation through the reaction of the scandalized subject. And the more the centrality of the other is absolute, ineluctable, the more this reaction tends toward violence. Hierarchical, in contrast with equalitarian, societies suffer the constant threat of internal revolt. They accumulate means to defend themselves; but these means are not always effective. Dynastic wars, with which wars of conquest and liberation are often associated, are far more serious affairs than the wars of primitive societies, which end most often by stabilizing themselves in a ritualized *quid pro quo*. And few dynastic wars do not have some prince's resentment as their point of departure.

Resentment thus exercises tremendous power in hierarchical society. Yet this power is ethically sterile, merely replacing one center with another while changing nothing essential in the structure of human relations. For resentment is a negative revelation. In the apparent closure of the center, the resentful party finds, or creates, an opening; what his rival does, he too can do. But even if he succeeds in his effort, the center will again be closed. The man of resentment is not powerless, but he creates nothing new. Resentment only distributes throughout the society the revelation that the first big-man transmitted in a direct line to his successors. But if resentment is ethically unproductive, it is nonetheless of enormous importance for the individual. The existence of a single central figure in society is the necessary and sufficient condition for all its members to acquire, in the full sense of the term, an individual self.

The human being is not conceivable without a self who aspires to the center. The doctrine of the "soul" is found in all the great religions (for example, the Hindu *atman* who aspires to union with the *brahman*). It is only another way of saying that man's *sine qua non* is his possession of language. The self as emitter of language must understand his peripheral status with respect to the scenic center to which the linguistic sign refers, and toward which his desire tends. Until the advent of hierarchical society, however, this desire remains imaginary; it gives rise to no action nor even to a conception of potential action. The aborted gesture, in designating the object, extends itself imaginarily toward it, but this extension remains a mere wish-fulfillment. When the participant in the scene finally arrives at the center to share the object with his fellows, he will have learned the great lesson, never to be forgotten by primitive society, that the center belongs not to the individual but to the community.

In daring individually to occupy the center, the big-man forges for himself an individuality unattainable by primitive man. But this individuality cannot remain a private possession; it is propagated throughout the society by means of resentment. Each of the leader's potential rivals discovers through his rivalry his own potential centrality. The individual human being acquires the ability to reconstitute the world imaginarily around himself. No doubt this reconstitution remains bound by the ethical sterility of the hierarchical social structure; the dream of the peripheral man is simply to change places with the central man. But even on this basis each is able to conceive himself as unique. In primitive society each preserves his symmetrical difference, but this difference remains a structural element, a function within the group. The individual's being is never distinguished from that of the preceding holders of the same function; in death, he will go to join the ancestors from whom he has never been essentially differentiated. In hierarchical society, even if successive kings or pharaohs perform *grosso modo* the same social function, they want to be recognized individually, historically. And in Egypt as early as the Middle Kingdom, the cult of Osiris offered to all the individualized immortality that the pyramids had conferred on the ancient pharaohs.

The creation of the individual is the greatest achievement of resentment. Resentment is the first sign of individuality. But this change in the relationship between the person and the scene of representation cannot lead to the ethical transcendence of archaic hierarchy until the scene has become the locus of a new, liberating revelation. The opening of the center to individuality permitted by the archaic religions remains always of the same order as that of the primitive scene. The gods of Egypt or of Assyria have more highly evolved technical functions than primitive deities, their exploits are told in a more subtle language, written as well as spoken. But their animal attributes and the fantastic nature of their adventures suffice to show that they are still nearer to Arunta gods than to the Hebrew God. The "secondary revelation" liberated enormous forces for the mastery of the natural world, and aroused in the individual a dream of centrality that makes each human being a potential god. But the meaning of this centrality itself had not evolved. Individuality could only express itself through such things as imitation of royal funeral customs, where the monumental certainty of entering into history was replaced by more accessible magical consolations.

The equality of all before the scene of representation is the most fundamental achievement of the originary revelation, one that no hierarchy can undo. But to seek such equality beyond death is to locate it in a place from which no revelation can ever issue forth. To adore the center in the form of one god or other according to the current dynastic power-relationships is to submit to the power emanating from the scene as though it derived from an external and alienated force. Akhenaton's "henotheistic" attempt at religious reform could not go beyond the establishment of a supreme cosmic power. Egyptian culture was unable to build on this foundation; it had too much to lose. The first great historical revelation would occur on the margins of archaic empire, within an enslaved people whose sole chance of survival lay in their liberation from the yoke of the hierarchical order.

NOTES

1. In his anthropological *magnum opus,* Les Formes élémentaires de la vie religieuse (4th ed., Paris: PUF, 1960), Durkheim gives this name to the Australian people known to modern ethnologists as the Arunta.

2. In *The Origin of Language* (Berkeley: University of California Press, 1981), I suggest that the evolution of these "elementary linguistic structures" must have taken place outside the public space of communal ritual. The new structures must first have appeared as aberrant usages of the old. But it would serve no useful purpose to describe the intuition of the individual who began to use them in this way as a "revelation," since the only communicable content of this intuition would be precisely the new linguistic form itself.

3. Chicago: Aldine-Atherton, 1972.

4. Scheler's little work *Über Ressentiment und moralisches Werturteil (On Resentment and Moral Value-Judgment)* (Leipzig: W. Engelmann, 1912), is better known in its expanded post-war version *Vom Umsturz der Werte (On the Overturning of Values),* Leipzig: Der Neue Geist, 1919).

3
The Mosiac Revelation

THE ORIGINARY HYPOTHESIS and the biblical text of the Mosaic revelation are mutually illuminating. Moses' solitary encounter on the mountain reproduces the structure of the hypothetical scene of origin. But the presence of the sacred being is no longer material; its only sign is the divine voice heard at the center of attention. The source of the words is Other, but there is no need to attribute this otherness to either supernatural or psychopathological causes; the Other has been from the beginning a constituent part of the Self. This text in which the divine Other reveals its non-figurality is the model for all subsequent texts of revelation.

The relationship between the Hebrews and their Egyptian masters—a captive minority within a dominant majority, a people of egalitarian nomads within a hierarchical empire—is paradigmatic of the resentful opposition of the periphery to the center that pervades all hierarchical societies. The Exodus is the exemplary liberation from the restrictiveness of the negative revelation of resentment. But this liberation cannot be understood independently of its theological ground. The Mosaic revelation created a historical watershed that separates a still living religion and its offshoots from cults long since defunct. To contest the triumph of Hebrew monotheism would be to deny the evidence of the spiritual dominance established over virtually the entire world by its heritage: Judaism, Christianity, Islam, Marxism; and this denial itself would only be conceivable on the basis of the opening bequeathed by the Hebrews to Western civilization.

The Centrality of the Mosaic Revelation in the Biblical Text

Nothing in the Bible formally marks the founding significance of the revelation on Mount Horeb. In Jewish tradition, it is the accomplishment of the Exodus that is the marked event, not the revelation that prepares it. The Hebrew Bible is the product of an established religion that presents the ultimate foundation of its belief as anterior to any historical revelation. The God who reveals himself to Moses is already presumed known to us as the creator of man and the world. But nothing in the story of the creation, nor even in that of the covenant with Abraham (which is surely not entirely bereft of historical foundation), should make us hesitate to attribute to the Mosaic revelation the role of a generative nucleus, of a historical point of departure. For just as the Bible, and the Jewish people, could never have come into existence without the Exodus, so the Exodus could never have taken place without the revelation on Horeb.

The biblical narrative of this revelation was not composed by an eyewitness, and it includes some evidently fabulous elements. Why then should we lend credence to this narrative when those of the basket among the bulrushes or the staff changed into a snake can only be read as legendary fables?

A discourse may be called *autoprobatory* if it describes something that must have taken place in order for the discourse to have been composed. We may claim with a high degree of probability that a text that gives an accurate description of, say, an elephant derives from the experience of an elephant, whether or not the experience is that of the text's author. But the description of a revelation is *necessarily* autoprobatory. One might arguably be able to imagine an elephant independently of worldly experience; but whether the content of a revelation is "real" or "imaginary" is an empty question, since the scene of representation is at once real and imaginary. Insofar as the report of the revelatory experience contains a new understanding of human relations, this understanding must really have occurred, whether or not in the context described. But the originary hypothesis further suggests that the experience cannot simply be separated from its context, since the scene on which it takes place, whether experienced in reality, imagined, or invented, derives from the originary event. Where the believer claims that God has spoken, the scoffer alleges hallucination or fraud. But the ethical understanding contained in a revelation depends on the recreation of the originary scene, however achieved, because the scene is the origin of human relations and the understanding it provides is the central source of our understanding of these relations. Thus the autoprobatory content of a discourse of revelation is not confined to what we might prefer to see as its universalizable anthropological content; it includes its scenic context as well. The revelatory scene corroborates a fundamental principle of generative anthropology: that no understanding of man can abstract from the particularity of his emergence in a specific event.

Conversely, the touchstone of an authentic narrative of revelation is that it contains an autoprobatory textual kernel that allows itself to be stripped of all secondary elements, fantastic or realistic, of referential description. We shall see that the narrative of Exodus 3 conforms to this criterion. We agree on this point with the affirmation of Martin Buber, a reader preeminent for his knowledge of the texts and for the strength of his religious intuition, and whose analysis will serve us as a guide throughout this chapter: ". . . such discoveries or conversions are not born at the writing desk. A speech like this . . . does not belong to literature but to the sphere attained by the founders of religion. If it is theology, it is that archaic theology which, in the form of a historical narrative, stands at the threshold of every genuine historical religion. No matter who related that speech or when, he derived it from a tradition which, in the last resort, cannot go back to anybody other than the founder."[1]

At the start of Exodus 3, Moses is in the country of Midian, where he has fled after having killed an Egyptian who was beating a Hebrew laborer. The Hebrews had long been slaves in Egypt. The text implies that Moses belongs to a superior social stratum; his depiction as the adopted grandson of the Pharaoh (Exodus 2.10) may indicate his assimilation into Egyptian society. His objection to God in 4.10, "I am a slow speaker and not able to speak well" may even be a reference to his difficulty with the Hebrew language. But to go as far as Freud's hypothesis that Moses was a princely Egyptian follower of Akhenaton would contradict both the text (where God reveals himself to Moses at the outset as "the God of your father," 3.6)[2] and all plausibility. The monotheism of the Hebrew God is compatible with the primitive religion of a nomadic people whose deity would have been attached to no polytheistic pantheon; on the other hand, it is not at all compatible with the "henotheism" of Akhenaton. To again quote Buber, "The universal sun-god of the imperialist "monotheism" of Amenhotep IV is incomparably more close to the national sun-god of the ancient Egyptian Pantheon than to the God of early Israel, which some [perhaps referring to Freud] have endeavoured to derive from him." (*Moses*, p. 8). As errant herdsmen reduced to quasi-slavery, the Hebrews may well have maintained a more or less egalitarian primitive religion; the more sophisticated Egyptian religious spirit could not escape from the constraints of hierarchical society. The historically new has often been seen to emerge not from what was most advanced in the old order, but from a marginal element, at once less differentiated and less favored, and thereby more open to change. In neglecting this tendency, Freud is curiously at one with Marx, who anticipated that socialism would emerge in the most advanced capitalist societies.

Here is the text of the Mosaic revelation. We make use here as elsewhere of the translation of the Jerusalem Bible (New York: Doubleday, 1966).

Exodus 3

> [1]Moses was looking after the flock of Jethro, his father-in-law, priest of Midian. He led his flock to the far side of the wilderness and came to

Horeb, the mountain of God. ²There the angel of Yahweh appeared to him in the shape of a flame of fire, coming from the middle of a bush. Moses looked; there was the bush blazing, but it was not being burnt up. ³"I must go and look at this strange sight," Moses said "and see why the bush is not burnt." ⁴Now Yahweh saw him go forward to look, and God called to him from the middle of the bush. "Moses, Moses!" he said. "Here I am" he answered. ⁵"Come no nearer" he said. "Take off your shoes, for the place on which you stand is holy ground. ⁶I am the God of your father," he said "the God of Abraham, the God of Isaac, and the God of Jacob." At this Moses covered his face, afraid to look at God. ⁷And Yahweh said, "I have seen the miserable state of my people in Egypt, I have heard their appeal to be free of their slave-drivers. Yes, I am well aware of their sufferings. ⁸I mean to deliver them out of the hands of the Egyptians and bring them up out of that land to a land rich and broad, a land where milk and honey flow, the home of the Canaanites, the Hittites, the Amorites, the Perizzites, the Hivites and the Jebusites. ⁹And now the cry of the sons of Israel has come to me, and I have witnessed the way in which the Egyptians oppress them, ¹⁰so come, I send you to Pharaoh to bring the sons of Israel, my people, out of Egypt." ¹¹Moses said to God, "Who am I to go to Pharaoh and bring the sons of Israel out of Egypt?" ¹²"I shall be with you," was the answer "and this is the sign by which you shall know that it is I who have sent you... After you have led the people out of Egypt, you are to offer worship to God on this mountain." ¹³Then Moses said to God, "I am to go, then, to the sons of Israel and say to them, 'The God of your fathers has sent me to you.' But if they ask me what his name is, what am I to tell them?" ¹⁴And God said to Moses, "I Am who I Am. *[ehyeh asher ehyeh]* This" he added "is what you must say to the sons of Israel: 'I Am has sent me to you.'" ¹⁵And God also said to Moses, "You are to say to the sons of Israel: 'Yahweh, the God of your fathers, the God of Abraham, the God of Isaac, and the God of Jacob, has sent me to you.' This is my name for all time; by this name I shall be invoked for all generations to come."

The God who reveals himself here takes on no corporeal appearance. It is his angel, his messenger who takes the form of the "flame of fire"; when God calls Moses "from the middle of the bush" it is only by his *word* that he is manifested. The flame as his messenger designates the locus of the revelatory event. Might this be the actual occasion of the Mosaic revelation? We may give this burning bush that "was not being burnt up" the obvious symbolic meaning of the eternal flame of the ancestral faith, whose violence preserves rather than destroys. But the flame is not merely symbolic; it recalls the fire that serves in ritual feasts to cook the meat of the sacrifice. This postponement of satisfaction recreates the configuration of the primordial revelation. Moses' awaiting by the fire reproduces the awaiting that must have taken place around the central object of the first designative gesture. But in the place of the appetitive reinforcement provided by the sacrificial meat, what Moses is awaiting is spiritual nourishment, the solution to his and his people's dilemma. Whether symbol or real experience, the bush provides a plausible circumstance for the revelation that will follow.

Until God speaks to Moses, the narrative remains linked to the symbols and realities of primitive religion. For the new revelation must link up with the essence of the old. The bush that burns without being consumed is nothing miraculous in itself: perhaps certain shrubs take longer to burn than others. Must we presume, with certain commentators, that there existed a specific cult on this mountain, whether of the fire, of the bush, or of the mountain itself? None of this is impossible; yet the experience recounted here cannot be subsumed under any previously established cult. For Moses' solitude is necessary, particularly his moral solitude. This passage cannot recount the disguised experience of a participant or a witness of a tribal rite. Such reductive explanations reflect the familiar fear of the event. The presumed "cult of the bush" would be a typical primitive religion; this primitive cult would then be called upon to generate the Hebrew religion by the same kind of eventless slippage that we have criticized in the ahistorical "scenarios" of the origin of language.

The sacrificial fire's consumption of fuel anticipates man's material consumption of the food it helps prepare. Here the fire does not burn for consumption's sake; it maintains itself, and thus maintains the attention of Moses until it becomes a source of speech. It is a ritual center that has become the locus of a revelatory opening. The first words translate the centripetal/centrifugal tension that has characterized the center from the beginning: the call that attracts the attention of the peripheral spectator ("Moses, Moses!") and the requirement that he maintain his distance from it ("Come no nearer"). The fire too is something that fascinates, that attracts attention, but that may not be approached too closely. The next sentence, which affirms the holiness of the place, only makes explicit the sanctity of the forbidden central locus.

Moses' first reply, "Here I am," is fundamental to the phenomenon of revelation. The revelatory experience must begin with the affirmation of the presence of the self, for it is on the basis of this presence, the only datum that is absolutely necessary and at the same time absolutely autoprobatory, that Moses understands the truth of the revelation as *his* truth.[3] In opposition to the hypothetical originary revelation, that of Moses is a solitary experience of a kind available only to a self individualized by the trial of resentment. Moses has already passed through the ordeal of the negative revelation, where the "Here I am" is a forced admission of presence before the scandalous centrality of the Other. His killing of the Egyptian testifies to the intensity of this experience. Now, on the contrary, "Here I am" is a voluntary affirmation which for that very reason expresses a new variety of presence. What is seen in the bush is not a figure, but the absence of all figures, the expression of a force that does not exhaust itself in the material world because its field of operation is not limited to the worldly rhythms of growth and death that govern primitive ritual.

The "God of your father" is that of Moses' ancestors. Moses has distanced himself from his ancestral rites; the sight of the fire provokes an intuition of return. For him to see in it the locus of the sacred does not require him to rediscover a long-lost memory, not even that of legend. On the contrary, the intuition of the equivalence between the sacred of one's ancestors and so curious an apparition could no doubt only occur to a man without any such concrete memory. The experience of return is liberating just because this fire is not a feature of current ritual practice; this primitive, figureless center is a rejection of the altars of Egyptian religion, crowded with alien deities that offer no protection for his people. Moses shields his face out of fear to look upon God. In refusing to see now that he hears the voice, he assures himself of figural emptiness. The non-figurality of God is equivalent in practice to Moses' refusal to fix his gaze. Had he stared at the fire, the flame would no doubt have passed from the status of a preparatory symbol, of a messenger angel, into that of the figure of a pre-Mosaic deity.

Whatever Moses' past may have been, his present experience can only be understood in relation to his future role as the liberator of his people. The Hebrews are a marginal population enslaved by Egypt, and the revelation is in the first place the instrument of their liberation. This is emphasized in the first long discourse of the divine voice (3.7-10). Moses can learn nothing new from it about the condition of the Hebrews; revelation is not a source of worldly information. What he learns is his responsibility toward them. Insofar as this people has retained its identity, it need not remain submerged by Egyptian military and cultural power, but can rise up against it. No doubt such uprisings can be undertaken only in favorable circumstances, on the subject of which the biblical text is not a very sure guide. But that the Hebrews may have been aided by extrinsic political or economic factors does not reduce their revolt to a simple *coup de force*. Nor is their departure a mere return to ancestral life. Interpreting the God of their ancestors in a radically new way, the Hebrew people will not return to its primitive nomadic state. It will establish a structured society in a new land, one that will evolve into an ever-problematic monarchy. With its ethical roots in an acephalous, tribal society, Mosaic religious culture will pursue its future maturation through the prophetic critique of a hierarchical system that can never remain altogether faithful to its origins.

But what is important for the moment is not the creation of a new society, but the rejection of a scandalous submission. The Hebrews' resentment must be transformed by the Mosaic revelation into a creative force before it can engender a new social order. The resentful "anti-revelation" sees in the scenic center only the liberty that already exists there. A prince replaces a prince, a state replaces a state, while the basic structure remains unchanged. Under Moses' direction the Hebrews will break the circle; but the origin of their strength is in resentment, as the discourse of 3.7-10 makes clear. It is no accident that the liberation of Israel from the hands of the Egyptians is first presented in terms of conquest. Here the promised land is neither that of the ancestors nor that earlier promised to Abraham (Genesis 17.8), but "a land rich and broad, . . . the home of the Canaanites, the Hittites, the Amorites. . ." Certainly the kingdom of Israel, even at the height of its glory, would never be comparable to the Egyptian empire—geography would not permit it—and Israel's accomplishments would never be measurable by the conquest and enslavement of other peoples. But the first part of the revelation breathes a desire for domination; liberation is first conceived within the symmetry of resentment.

Moses' first intuition of his role as leader is followed by a moment of doubt. The revelatory dialogue that takes up the rest of this passage will alternate between doubt and divine reassurance. The dialogic structure is essential; it mirrors the oscillatory communication between the peripheral self and the central Other in the originary scene. The resistance of the central object to the desire it engenders on the periphery makes it the source of the meaning of the designative gesture. As it was at the origin, the divine center's resistance to human desire is the theological heart of revelation.

Until this point Moses has heard a promise of liberation based on return to his ancestral God. The symbolism of the bush suggests that this God is no mere symmetrical rival of the gods of the Egyptian pantheon in their function of alimentary redistribution. The God of the ancestors has become the center of a possibility of renewal and liberation that Moses will have to communicate to the other Hebrews. Now that this intuition has been reached, the question is posed, "Who am I . . . ?" Moses asks who he is insofar as he is a person (re)defined by revelation. Here again the text is autoprobatory. God's answers are those of the new center from which Moses shields his face. What he must do is concentrate on this opening or clearing of the center in the hope of hearing a discourse that will maintain the opening. The words attributed to God express a series of intuitions of the truths that the presence of this central opening makes accessible.

The first answer is a guarantee of the divine presence: "I shall be with you." The promised "sign" is that the people will return to the same mountain to render a cult to God. A doubtful passage, but one that may be explained at least hypothetically by the continuity of the divine presence until the liberation. The guarantee of God's presence cannot be a mere magical "sign" like the staff/snake that is a degraded addition to the revelatory experience. The only real sign of the power of the Mosaic revelation—as of all revelation—is its collective effectiveness. If the renewed worship of the God of their ancestors does not succeed in liberating the Hebrew people, his revelation to Moses will be "falsified" and will not become history. The revealed truth is a truth for man that remains without effect so long as it has not become the point of departure for a new system of human relations. Yet what can be done with a "sign" that can only manifest itself after the fact? The "sign by which you shall know that it is I who have sent you" is not something that Moses will be able to show to the Hebrews as a guarantee of his election. This sign is for the moment only a *hypothesis*, the hypothesis that Moses will have to keep in mind throughout the performance of his task. It is thus the equivalent of "I shall be with you," which uses the same word *(ehyeh)* as the "I am" of verse 14. The being-with of God promises that the meaning of the revelation will endure;

the worship rendered on the mountain after the liberation will be the confirmation of this promise.

The response to the "Who am I?" of Moses is the hypothetical being-with of revealed truth, or in other words, of faith. Moses cannot define himself before the revelation otherwise than by faith. For this is an individual experience, cut off from immediate confirmation by the community. Like the first big-man, Moses is a chosen individual—a fact sufficient to demonstrate that the new communal structure he will found will not be able to effect a simple return to primitive equality.

The Name of God

The last part of the quoted passage contains the theological high point of the Mosaic revelation. That this moment of greatest originality is found at the end rather than at the beginning only confirms the dialectical authenticity of the biblical narrative. The specific character of the Hebrew God may be said to be determined by his promise of liberation. But this theological truth is not simply given, nor is it deduced from an interpretation of the sign of the burning bush. It is worked out in the course of the dialogue between Moses and God. Nothing supernatural intervenes in this dialogue; the divine voice manifests itself in/to Moses in response to his attempt to flesh out the primary intuition inspired by the bush.

For it is one thing to hear a messenger of his ancestral God bearing a promise of return to independence, and another to make this promise effective for his people. Moses is not a theologian speculating at leisure on the divine substance; he wants to know the name of God in order to be able to mobilize the Hebrews *in his name*. If the reply to his question contains what we may call without exaggeration the greatest theological lesson of all time, it is because the nature of his mission required such a lesson. The socio-political oppression of the Hebrews under the Egyptian yoke is paradigmatic of the subordination not merely of one people to another but of all mankind to the negative revelation of resentment that dominates archaic hierarchical society. The solution of the Exodus is not merely a means for preserving national identity; it provides the ethical principle that will eventually permit the emergence of modern social systems. The hierarchical order of society is not abandoned, but it is clearly subordinated to the egalitarian morality of the originary scene. The Judeo-Christian tradition will interpret the entire course of history according to the model of the Exodus.

Moses asks in what name he is to speak to his people. What he appears to be seeking is the "magic" name of the ancestral God that will galvanize the energy of the faithful. Buber's gloss (p. 48-49) that the question "what is his name?" addresses the substance, the referent of the name rather than the name itself seems like a case of special pleading. Moses is no philosopher; his interest is practical rather than theoretical. That his question could not be answered by the simple production of a new or old name is demonstrated only after the fact, by the answer that it receives.

Ehyeh asher ehyeh, "I am who/what/that I am," is no doubt the most significant crux of biblical interpretation. Is God hiding behind a tautology; does he mean "I am he who is," he on whom all being is founded? The challenge is all the greater for an interpretation that seeks in revelation an anthropological truth. The problem is not to know "what God meant to say," but to understand how such a statement could have emerged in the mind of Moses as the only adequate answer to his question.

Buber insists (p. 52) on the necessity that this sentence have a meaning that is more than tautological. Emphasizing the existential sense of *ehyeh,* which is repeated three times in this passage, he would like to translate "I am and will remain present, in which I will be present." The present/future verb is repeated in the form of a tautology in order to demonstrate to Moses that his fears are unfounded, that God does not have to be evoked by means of a particular name, that he is a permanent presence that no evocation can influence. In Buber's analysis, this interpretation follows the discussion of the name "Yahweh" or "YHVH," although this name mentioned only at the end of the biblical text. The reason for this is clear: despite the refinement of his religious intuition, Buber remains enclosed in a theological mode of thought. He explains God's words not in their real order, but in the logical order of the rational mental processes one would attribute to an anthropomorphic God. For God would certainly be expected to know his own name, which is not *ehyeh asher ehyeh,* nor the simple *ehyeh* of the following sentence, but YHVH. God would intentionally reveal his name only once he has given an interpretation of it:

> And it is the God Himself who unfolds his name after this fashion. The exclamation [Yahweh] was its hidden form; the verb [ehyeh] is its revelation. And in order to make it clear beyond all possibility of misapprehension that the direct word *ehyeh* explains the indirect name, Moses is first instructed, by an exceptionally daring linguistic device, to tell the people "*Ehyeh,* I shall be present, or I am present, sends me to you," and immediately afterwards: "YHVH the God of your fathers sends me to you." (Buber, p. 53)

But as soon as the will of God is made to serve as an explanation given prior to the dialogue rather than emerging within it, the revelation loses its experiential quality. The voice comes to Moses "from without," but we can understand its utterances only on the basis of intuitions aroused in him by his nascent understanding of the theological preconditions for religious and political liberation.

The sentence is remarkable for its gnomic character. Its symmetry makes it particularly appropriate for oral transmission; if Moses left an "oral law" behind him, it is surely these words that would have had the best chance of being handed down unaltered to the drafters of the text of Exodus. However we may prefer to read the sentence, even as Buber's "I am (will be) present, but only insofar as I myself will be present" (that is, independently of the desires of those who seek to evoke me), this formal symmetry cannot be exhausted by any particular reading. For the words of the sentence are at the same time an answer to the request for the *name* of God.

God has just employed *ehyeh* in the sentence "I shall be with you. . ." Here is already revealed the permanence of the divine presence, which is at the same time its independence from any specific ritual locus. But Moses wonders how this presence can be evoked before the people. *Ehyeh asher ehyeh* emerges then, not as a proleptic gloss on the name YHVH, but as an intensification of God's preceding sentence that is at the same time a refusal of his concrete name. It is the presence itself that will be present, in the sense of a central being purged of all figurality. The relative pronoun *asher,* which can signify "that" as well as "that which," should be read here in an even freer sense: "I am" is linked only with "I am," and this tautological bond embraces all possible relationships. For the intuition expressed in this symmetrical statement is that the presence of God does not refer back to a name, but only to itself. "I am what I am" and "I am that which is" are only two partial readings that we may extract from the more general truth that the presence of the scenic center is independent of all place and of all figure, that it is the sole presence before which man exists as man, but that for as long as he remains a member of mankind—for as long as he accepts his ethical responsibility to his community, for as long as he continues to say "here I am"—this presence will not abandon him. In place of the specifying name, Moses encounters the omnipresent self-determination of the "monotheistic" God.

In this manner the Mosaic revelation breaks through the confining symmetry of resentment. It is no longer a matter of replacing the Egyptian gods by another god, even if he be unique, but of substituting for the center closed by the rival Other an open center that is a pure locus of presence. The name is the means of invoking God, but what does the invocation of God really mean in anthropological terms? Naming God is the sense of the originary signifying act directed towards the central object. This gesture is *ostensive;* it designates its referent by showing it. To name God outside the communal scene is to give the name an *imperative* sense by summoning him to appear in order to reconstitute this scene. A name is an imperative/ostensive, as its vocative use makes clear.⁴ But what God replies to Moses here is not a name, but a *declarative sentence,* an utterance that neither designates a particular center like the ostensive nor attempts, like the imperative, to reconstitute it. The declarative does not refer directly to the world; it constructs a model of the world on the internal scene of representation that all men have inherited from the originary event. The God whose "name" is a declarative sentence makes himself accessible only as spirit.

These three categories—ostensive, imperative, declarative—comprise the three stages of linguistic evolution proposed in *The Origin of Language*. In the argument of that work, the declarative sentence, the emergence of which corresponds to the "linguistic maturity" characteristic of all historically known languages, first appears as a negative reply to an imperative utterance, a reply that serves to inform the speaker of the imperative that the object he is demanding is unavailable and must be sought elsewhere. Such a sentence can only become a successful mode of communication if the speaker of the original imperative is willing to accept, in the place of the presence of the object that the imperative had requested, a *conceptual* scene on which the object can be imagined as present. The imperative is a "magic" mode of speech that expects the utterance of the sign to produce its counterpart in reality through the agency of its hearer; the declarative reply substitutes information for performance, a conceptual object for a worldly one.

When this object is divine, the declarative is an expression of "negative theology." But the sentence by which God answers Moses is, despite its tautological character, affirmative. It affirms the permanence of the imaginary scene as a prerequisite not only of linguistic communication, but above all of human relations. The God who "is what he is" is the God who exists only to maintain an imaginary scene purged of any preconceived central object. This first god to guarantee the ontological necessity of the declarative sentence guarantees man's freedom to engage in thought beyond the ideological bounds of hierarchical society, a freedom that the prophets would later reaffirm against the very social order that the Exodus had made possible. God's sentence teaches Moses that at the center of the communal scene, where the old hierarchical society still preserved the memory of an originary figure, there must exist only a free place. Far from being an interpretation of the name YHVH, the sentence *ehyeh asher ehyeh* reveals by its very syntactical construction the irrelevance of all divine names. This is the summit of the Mosaic revelation.

Let us examine more closely the intuition that opened up the passage from the asked name to the answered sentence. This sentence is affirmative, for it affirms the presence, not the absence, of God. The revelatory leap will appear more comprehensible if we remark that in the context of the dialogue up to this point, the content of this sentence, its contribution of new information in relation to what precedes, is nil. God having already affirmed his future presence at Moses's side, this sentence only twice reaffirms this presence. It is thus not unreasonably interpreted as "I am what I am," or in other words, "my essence is inaccessible to any names that you might pronounce." It is only on the basis of this refusal that the positive contribution of the sentence can appear. The "I am" is linked only to the "I am"; but this bond reinvests the sentence with content, for it defines God's absence—his absence with respect to man's desire for a name by which to invoke him—in terms of his presence. The significance of this absence/presence goes beyond the theological domain. The declarative sentence, here as in the general case, designates an absence; but it is only within the framework of this absence, that is, within the scene of imaginary or conceptual representation guaranteed by the inaccessibility of the desired object, that the *truth* of the object, and objective truth in general, can manifest itself.

In the relation between man and God as Moses found it, we are not yet in the realm of truth but in that of desire. To call on a god, to give him the order to appear, is to make of him an object of desire—a desire that can be equally well individual as collective, that can express itself in a magical practice as well as in a communal rite. God's refusal reveals his absence from the center constituted by desire, but only in order to indicate the permanence of his presence. The sentence "I am who I am" can thus also be read "I am he who am—he who is present in the first person." This presence is an "absence" insofar as it reinterprets the originary presence of the central object on the originary scene of representation. The center no longer offers a concrete focus for desire; it has become a pure locus of spirit. God as the source of being is he who answers no to our desire to possess him, but whose refusal guarantees the objectivity of being as well as its accessibility to conceptual thought; we can only learn its truth on the condition that we respect its autonomy.

It is the transcendence of the stage of resentment, of the "negative revelation," that requires such an answer to Moses' question. A god who was a mere rival of the Egyptian gods could not have permitted a truly new opening. Such a god would have operated with the same means as his enemies; he could only conquer if the Hebrews were able to impose his worship by force, which was of course far from being the case. The deepest theological-ethical insight of the Bible, as displayed in the deutero-Isaic passages where Israel's sufferings are described as the sign of its election, is that the power of the Mosaic God cannot be measured by the worldly triumphs of his partisans. His presence is independent of victory and defeat, of the material satisfactions and sufferings of his people. And it is precisely for this reason that only this God can guarantee to the community of his believers a new kind of victory, a national liberation.

A religion is in the first place an ethic. Belief in a God endowed with magical powers along the lines of the Egyptian gods can be effective only in a society of the Egyptian type. Such gods, in contrast to the God of Moses, can give concrete guarantees of their power when they are called upon; but their divine power is equated with the secular power of their believers and cannot outlive the social organization they dominate. In contrast, the God of pure presence is invulnerable to changes in worldly conditions. Because his believers can remain faithful to him even when oppressed by their enemies, these believers have declared themselves in advance independent of the social order that subjugates them. In worshipping such a God even while obeying their Egyptian masters, the Hebrews would have been able to maintain a spiritual freedom that these masters must have found scandalous and subversive.

But this "subversion" also had practical consequences. The ten plagues, like the plague at Thebes in the *Oedipus,* are best seen as disorders less natural than human, disorders in which the Hebrews themselves may conceivably have played a part. But whatever grain of truth the episode of the plagues contains, it suffices to observe that a people for whom God is the objective source of being-in-general is better adapted to a reality in crisis than one whose gods are only the guarantors of an order that remains under its control. Seen in this light, the narrative of the Exodus may be disencumbered of its fantastic elements. The Hebrews, mobilized by the Mosaic faith, must have become indocile slaves. Pharaoh, perhaps motivated by difficulties that rendered their services less useful, was willing, perhaps even glad, to rid himself of a people that had become fundamentally, because religiously, disloyal. The new faith may have begun to serve as a principle of communal organization even before the final abandonment of Egyptian territory. The core of the Mosaic legislation—for example, the requirement of Sabbath rest—may well date from the time of the Exodus. What is more certain is that the equality before God prescribed by the new faith, in contrast to the ritual equality of primitive societies, was strong enough to maintain the solidarity of a community in crisis that must have maintained at all times a considerable degree of hierarchical structure.

Let us examine one last time the sentence *ehyeh asher ehyeh*. The presence of God to Moses is the guarantee of the well-foundedness of his enterprise of liberation. Why then was Moses unable to give him a name? It is not merely unlikely that he had forgotten the name of the God of his ancestors, it is irrelevant whether he had or not. The symmetry of the declarative sentence was able to come to him only in answer to the demand for a new name, more powerful than the old. God's sentence frustrates the immediate question, but gives the questioner a qualitatively higher satisfaction. As a declarative rather than an ostensive, a statement rather than a magic word, it is a truth that can serve in all circumstances, a universal "name" more powerful than any name whose specificity allows it to function only within a given social order. The statement can be reaffirmed on any occasion, for which it supplies not an etiological explanation in the manner of myth but a universal theological justification the intersubjective force of which we cannot overestimate. This was the force that imposed the sentence in the revelatory dialogue.

The strength of ideas is always put to the test in the intersubjective situation of dialogue. For positive ideas, the real world supplies means of corroboration that can enter into this dialogue. But the dialogue itself is primary. Man's fundamental problem is always with his fellow man rather than with nature. Once this is understood, religious ideas are seen to be no more arbitrary than positive ones. They are in fact tested through the dialogue of historical experience more thoroughly than any others. The victory of the "higher" religions over primitive idolatry, or the success of religions of resentment in the third world today, cannot be explained by the mere force that inspires swordpoint conversions. The superior religion at a given moment possesses a superior truth that manifests itself in practice in the form of a superior *rhetoric*. Nietzsche and his deconstructive followers are correct to assert that, within the dialectic of human relations, the rhetorical is in the final analysis unsurmountable. Where they go wrong is in drawing from this truth the unwarranted conclusion that because rhetorical dialogue is not wholly determinable by logical principles it is simply undecidable. A viable anthropology must respect history; it should be neither formalistic nor merely empirical, and above all it should not be forced to choose between determinism and nihilism. We must accept—indeed, we should welcome—the fact that historical revelations are not deducible from a hypothesis of origin. The rhetorical nature of religious truth is a consequence of the urgency of man's need to create order and limit conflict, a need that is the very foundation for human as opposed to animal existence. Man requires revelation because he must make urgent ethical decisions in concrete situations, just as Moses is about to do in Exodus. Not even the truth of the revelation of monotheism is ever definitively established. History is made by the revelations that men have chosen to retain in preference to others, for never altogether sufficient reasons, and that they can always choose at some future date to reject.

Religious argument is determined not by deductive logic but by an intuition of rightness. The fact that this intuition is "subjective" does not, however, close it off to rational investigation. Religious intuition is not an ineffable mystery. It is open to study both from the perspective of its intrinsic operation (its "form") and from that of the actual results it produces (its "content"). The originary hypothesis offers a basis for understanding the form; our examination of the biblical content is made in the light of this prerequisite understanding.

The rhetorical point of God's reply to Moses is that this God whose being is omnipresent and self-determined cannot be evoked by the same logical class of statements as the primitive gods. If he had a name and a figure, this name and this figure would merely oppose themselves to the name and figure of other gods. But his "name" is the self-definition of his being. One has only to ask his name to receive the demonstration of his greater universality than the other gods whose namedness particularizes them. For one who sees the name of his god as a source of power, the reply would be at the very least disconcerting. But as a result of it the Hebrew God becomes *less falsifiable* than the Egyptian gods. His reign does not depend on practical results; his presence affirms itself independently of all human means of invocation.

It is nonetheless true that this God revealed himself to Moses with the goal of accomplishing a concrete act: leading the Hebrews out of Egypt. The rest of the passage, with its transition from the sentence *ehyeh asher ehyeh* to the name YHVH, is dominated by the strength of this necessity. But the theological, rhetorical, and quite simply the ethical force of the revelatory statement is not dissipated. God can promise a victory, he can give himself a name, without for all that being dependent either on that victory or on that name. Thus his sentence-name is given first, before he is forced to descend from the heights of revelation to more practical considerations. The prior understanding that their God is not named like the others will help his people to assure victory by their own efforts.

When the name was requested, the sentence was given. But the dialogue now moves toward the worldly necessity of the communication of the name to the people. This movement is both an advance toward the historical realization that alone can valorize and preserve the revelation and a retreat on the theological plane toward a less radical presentation of the new conception of the deity, a compromise that preserves the core of namelessness while satisfying the need for a name. The remainder of the conversation takes place without any further intervention on Moses' part. Having intuited the sentence as the most authentic reply to his question, he will now find in this sentence itself the name he had been seeking.

The sentence had presented itself without consideration for the communicative context to which Moses' question referred: ". . . but if they ask me what his name is . . ." Now God answers more specifically: "This is what you must say to the sons of Israel: I am *(ehyeh)* has sent me to you." The three-part sentence has been reduced to its essential verbal element, *ehyeh*. The "name" still remains a sentence, but a sentence consisting of a single word, which is thus ambiguously a sentence and a name. And in the following sentence, this ambiguity will be removed; it is YHVH, "the God of your fathers," who speaks.

Was the name YHVH already known to the Hebrews? It might seem difficult to doubt it. The text, however, affirms the contrary, implicitly here, and explicitly in the "sacerdotal" version of the revelation to be discussed below. But the question of the novelty of the name itself is of less importance than that of the novelty of its meaning. On this point, another passage from Buber corroborates both our interpretation of the biblical text, and, in a striking way, our originary anthropological hypothesis.

> Of all the various suppositions regarding the prehistoric use of the name YHVH there is only one the development of which makes all this understandable without contradiction. To the best of my knowledge it was first expressed nearly half a century ago by Duhm in an (unpublished) lecture at Goettingen: "Possibly the name is in some degree only an extension of the word *hu*, meaning "he," as God is also called by other Arab tribes at times of religious revival—the One, the Unnameable." The Dervish cry Ya-hu is interpreted to mean "O he!", and in one of the most important poems of the Persian mystic, Jelaluddin Rumi, the following occurs: "One I seek, One I know, One I see, One I call. He is the first, He is the last, He is the outward, He is the inward. I know no other except Yahu (O He) and Ya-man-hu (O-He-who-is)." The original form of the cry may have been *Ya-huva*, if we regard the Arabic pronoun *huwa*, he, as the original Semitic form of the pronoun "he," which, in Hebrew as well as in another Arabic form, has become *hu*. "The name *Ya-huva* would then mean O-he! with which the manifestations of the god would be greeted in the cult when the god became perceptible in some fashion. Such a *Ya-huva* could afterwards produce both *Yahu* and *Yahveh* (possibly originally *Yahvah*)." [Author's note: {The German Hebraist} Mowinckel, in a letter to Rudolf Otto, printed in R. Otto, *Das Gefuehl des Ueberweltlichen* (1932), p. 326f.] Similar divine names deriving from "primitive sounds" are also known in other religions, but in, say, the Dionysos cult the cries developed into corresponding nouns, whereas the Semites preserved the elemental cry itself as a name. Such a name, which has an

The Mosaic Revelation

> entirely oral character and *really requires completion by some such gesture as, for example, the throwing out of an arm,* [my emphasis] is, to be sure (as long, at least, as the undertone of the third person still affects the consciousness of speaker and listener) more suitable for evocation than for invocation. As an invocation it appears in the story of the patriarchs only in a cry (Genesis 49.18) which strangely interrupts the continuity of the blessings of Jacob. (Buber, pp. 49-50)

But this primitive name undergoes a change in meaning as a result of the Mosaic revelation:

> At the same time, however, [that religion is demagified], the meaning and character of the Divine Name itself changes; that is, from the viewpoint of the narrator as well as from that of the tradition given shape by him, it is unfolded in its true sense. By means of the introduction of an inconsiderable change in vocalization, a change to which the consciousness of sound would not be too sensitive, a wildly ecstatic outcry, half interjection half pronoun, is replaced by a grammatically precise verbal form which, in the third person (*havah* is the same as *hayah*—to be—but belongs to an older stratum of language) means the same as is communicated by the *ehyeh:* YHVH is "He who will be present" or "He who is here," he who is present here; not merely some time and some where but in every now and in every here. Now the name expresses his character and assures the faithful of the richly protective presence of their Lord. (Buber, p. 53)

It is impossible to see in the primitive name as described by Buber anything other than an *ostensive.* This name-cry that "really requires completion" by an accompanying gesture of designation is fully compatible with our description of the scene of the origin of language. That the ancient Hebrews had called their God by such a "name" would put their ritual practice close to the most primitive religious behavior. But we should doubt whether this cry was *the name itself* of the archaic Hebrew God. The ecstatic cry of the Persian mystic is not after all the name of his God. By modifying Buber's hypothesis we can deepen the theological and anthropological lesson of the revelation of the divine name, while remaining at the same time more faithful to the biblical text, which affirms the novelty of this name.

The primitive name of the Hebrew God may very well have been forgotten, if not in Moses' day, then by the time of composition of the Torah. El Shaddai, which the "sacerdotal" narrative affirms to have been the pre-Mosaic name, is more properly a title, and the other biblical designation, Elohim, is a generic plural. This omission becomes more understandable if we suppose that the name revealed to and by Moses was not altogether new. We may presume that the cry cited by Duhm/Mowinckel was not the usual name of God, but an ecstatic way of designating his central apparition in the rite—in sum, an ostensive. From this cry, by means of something like the vocal change suggested by Buber, Moses extracted a new name that preserved, to the extent that any name can do so, the meaning of the revelation that he had just received. It is fully plausible that the God who says "I am" be designated by a name that means "he who is." Since it was necessary for God to inspire his people to practical action, since a name was therefore inevitable, the choice was the least nominative name possible, the name that would maximally preserve the revelation of non-figural substance expressed in the verb "to be." To take a "cry" for a name is also to grasp that the original name of God could only have been such a cry, that the higher linguistic forms that permit the worshipper to refer to God outside his presence to the community are products of later, less crucial moments. The name-cry reproduces the designation of the sacred center in the originary scene: ecstatic awareness of timeless presence with no thought of individual magical invocation.

The difference between this interpretation and Buber's is that it situates the passage from the ostensive ("Ya-hu!") to the verbal name (YHVH) that recalls the declarative sentence no longer in a forgotten history to be reconstructed by philologists, but *within the revelatory experience itself.* For Buber, the change of vocalization and meaning carried

The Mosaic Revelation

out by Moses can only be explained if the primitive meaning of the name/cry was already forgotten in Moses' time:

> Certainly it is more typical [than to think that the name attributed to Moses' mother, Jochebed, is the sign of a specific familial tradition linking Moses to the primitive name] that in the course of the ages, particularly at an epoch of increasing religious laxity, as the Egyptian period appears to have been for Israel, the element of excitation and discharge connected with the calling of the name did not merely ebb away, but the name itself degenerated into a sound simultaneously empty and half-forgotten. Under such conditions an hour might well come when the people would ask this question of a man bringing them a message from the God of their fathers: "How about his name?" That means: "What is this God really like? We cannot find out from his name!" (Buber, pp. 50-51)

This half-forgetting of the name is suspect: if the name were still known as a name, one would not ask its meaning. It is far simpler to assume that in this ostensive cry, whether still in use or not, Moses found the phonetic incarnation of his new message. Without making use of a concrete name, which could correspond only to a concrete figure, he transforms an ostensive that designated the manifest presence of God independently of any system of particular differences into a declarative expression that reveals God only as the subject of the verb *to be*. In becoming the symbol of the new "declarative" conception of God, the name YHVH integrates at the same time the ancient "ostensive" one that had remained unmodified at the core of religious experience throughout the edification of the great cosmological civilizations. This transcendental integration of the originary theology within the new, in opposition to the figural/magical gods of hierarchical society, supports the thesis that there have been only two truly fundamental revelations: that of the event at the origin of man and that of the burning bush, which gave birth to the conception of the one God that is shared by all Western religions and their secular derivatives.

The Exoteric Revelation

How did Moses communicate the liberating substance of this revelation to the Hebrew people? On this point, the text of Exodus hardly goes beyond the legendary. God gives Moses magical powers, which he uses not to convince his compatriots but to impress Pharaoh: at the same time, God hardens the latter's heart, apparently for the pleasure of prolonging the spectacle of his impotent rage. The series of improbable encounters between Moses and Pharaoh seems to have been conceived deliberately in order to avoid reference to the Hebrews' own contribution to the Exodus and to the crucial role played by Moses among the people whose leader he had become.

The text contains nonetheless a few valuable indications. The first and only account of the contact between Moses and his people before the Exodus is that of Chapter 5. Moses and Aaron have gone to see Pharaoh to ask him to let the Hebrews go into the desert to celebrate a holiday in honor of God. Pharaoh's response is to discontinue the delivery of straw to the brick makers. When the Hebrew foremen (some versions call them "scribes") complain to the monarch, they discover that the cause of his anger is the desire that he attributes to the Hebrews "to go and offer sacrifice to Yahweh." The foremen then turn against Moses and Aaron: "'May Yahweh see your work and punish you as you deserve!' they said to them. 'You have made us hated by Pharaoh and his court; you have put a sword into their hand to kill us'" (5.21). It is after this passage that God gives Moses the "sacerdotal" revelation of Exodus 6.

We note first of all that those who complain to Moses are not the workers themselves but their representatives before the Egyptians. The biblical text has Moses solicit the holiday from Pharaoh; but the anger of the latter and his court, as well as that of the foremen, becomes more understandable if we suppose that the request to celebrate YHVH came rather from below than from above. The Egyptians would have learned of this demand not from Moses but from the Hebrew people, who had been inspired to religious renewal by the revelation at Sinai. In this context, the "sacerdotal" narrative merits our attention.

This text is commonly treated as an alternative version of the revelation, but it appears in fact to refer to a later historical moment. God repeats in modified form his affirmations of Chapter 3:

Exodus 6

> ²God spoke to Moses and said to him, "I am Yahweh. ³To Abraham and Isaac and Jacob I appeared as El Shaddai; I did not make myself known to them by my name Yahweh. ⁴Also, I made my covenant with them to give them the land of Canaan, the land they lived in as strangers. ⁵And I have heard the groaning of the sons of Israel, enslaved by the Egyptians, and have remembered my covenant. ⁶Say this, then, to the sons of Israel, 'I am Yahweh. I will free you of the burdens which the Egyptians lay on you. I will release you from slavery to them, and with my arm outstretched and my strokes of power I will deliver you. ⁷I will adopt you as my own people, and I will be your God. Then you shall know that it is I, Yahweh your God, who have freed you from the Egyptians' burdens. ⁸Then I will bring you to the land I swore that I would give to Abraham, and Isaac, and Jacob, and will give it to you for your own; I, Yahweh, will do this!'" ⁹Moses told this to the sons of Israel, but they would not listen to him, so crushed was their spirit and so cruel their slavery. ¹⁰Yahweh then said to Moses, ¹¹"Go to Pharaoh, king of Egypt, and tell him to let the sons of Israel leave his land." ¹²But Moses answered to Yahweh's face: "Look," said he "since the sons of Israel have not listened to me, why should Pharaoh listen to me, a man slow of speech?" ¹³Yahweh spoke to Moses and Aaron and ordered them both to go to Pharaoh, king of Egypt, and to bring the sons of Israel out of the land of Egypt.

Here, in contrast with the earlier version, the novelty of God's name is specifically emphasized, along with the revelatory progression that it symbolizes. But the most significant change is in God's relationship with his people. Whereas his original promise of conquest had merely inverted the experience of the conquered, here he presents the acquisition of the promised land not as the spoliation of Canaanites, Hittites, and Amorites, but as the renewal of a previous covenant with Abraham, Isaac, and Jacob. Here God addresses Moses merely as a preacher; his words are in fact addressed through him to the people as a whole. The differences between the two texts reflect the transformation of the message of individual revelation into a public gospel. To the extent that there really do exist two traditions, the present text expresses an exoteric tradition that complements rather than contradicts the "esoteric" one of Chapter 3.

"I will adopt you as my own people, and I will be your God." These are strange words in the mouth of a tribal deity, even as the expression of the renewal of his covenant with Abraham. We may even wonder whether this covenant was known to Moses' audience; was it an old tradition half-forgotten and recalled, or was it constructed *post factum* from the Mosaic revelation? YHVH could have been the "God of the fathers" and even the God of Abraham without the existence of a territorial promise going back to ancient times. Only in the context of the Exodus will the promised land become the object of a historical project.

But if God's adoption of Israel can be revealed to the people only in the context of their departure from Egypt, the theological content of the Mosaic revelation lends this departure a broader meaning that makes of the liberation of this particular people the exemplary Exodus. Every tribal god is by definition the god of his people. But Israel is adopted by a God who is no longer tribal in any sense, who has become a self-perpetuating verbal and no longer figural being, the liberator of the ritual center. The present text touches only indirectly on this transformation, which the change of name from El Shaddai to YHVH suggests without explicitly affirming it. Although the *ehyeh asher ehyeh* has been preserved by tradition, there is no longer any mention of the sentence once it becomes necessary to address the Hebrew people.

We have supposed that this new name was not a really new one, but a ritual cry fallen into disuse. Although the name expresses the non-figural being of God, it is meant to be understood by the people in an ostensive sense. Under this gestural name, God adopts them for his own, requiring nothing of them other than an act of faith. The name YHVH is designed to arouse ecstatic adhesion, as before a ritually manifest deity. Yet when Moses pronounced these words, the children of Israel "would not listen to him." The divine order to go directly to Pharaoh prepares the narration of the plagues; revolution from above replaces revolution from below. God makes no answer to Moses' question as to why Pharaoh should receive him, and offers no explanation of how the king could be persuaded by one "slow of speech." In the place of an answer within the revelatory dialogue, we are given the plagues as effects of divine intervention. Only after the first nine plagues (and a number of interviews with Pharaoh), when it is a question of establishing the new rite of the Passover, does Moses again speak to the Hebrews, but to the "elders of Israel" alone (12.21). He will address the "people" only on the following day, when they will have already gone out from Egypt, commanding them to "keep this day in remembrance" (13.3).

Thus according to the biblical text, not only the original, esoteric revelation, but even the exoteric revelation specifically destined for transmission to the mass of the Hebrews could not be communicated. The biblical text does not present Moses as an effective orator until after God has revealed his worldly power to the people in the Exodus.

If Moses was indeed the historical leader of the Exodus, he must have been listened to far more often and far more passionately than appears in the biblical text. But if this text, following the autoprobatory narrative of the revelation, regresses to the level of miraculous legend, this cannot be because the people were unable to hear and follow Moses, but because the text is unable to *figure* this hearing. It would be altogether foreign to its purpose to depict a group of Hebrews applauding Moses' exhortations. The "people" in the Old Testament—and in the last analysis, those of the New as well—are never depicted as open to revelation but always as recalcitrant backsliders. Moses' failure as an orator is a justification of his authority as a prophetic leader. But more than this, textual authority is the correlative of ethical authority. The very authority of the biblical text that preserves the Mosaic revelation requires that the people be shown as incapable of grasping its message for themselves. This same representation of popular blindness to revelation is found in the New Testament. For the worldly success of a revelation, however great, can never be adequate to its truth, which cannot be the object of rational choice, but only of faith. God's rule, exercised here through Moses, must be grounded in authority and not in common consent. The Mosaic opening of the center promises equality before God, but not a return to primitive equalitarianism. The separation wrought by the big-man between the exchange of words and the exchange of things is not abolished—nor, despite appearances to the contrary, will it be abolished by Christianity. But now it is reestablished on an absolute theological foundation that will later serve to protect the freedom of prophetic discourse against the "ideological" temptation inherent in the monarchy.

The Hebrews would not listen to Moses "so crushed was their spirit and so cruel their slavery." The Hebrews are too oppressed to applaud Moses; the Mosaic revelation is too radical for them to comprehend, even if their eventual liberation gives proof of its effectiveness. Here we see the difference between the Hebrew and the Greek models of culture, between liberations public and private, real and fictitious, theophanic and esthetic. History has preserved the experience of Moses not because, like an artwork, it was memorable in itself, but because it was effective. The Jewish Passover celebrates to this day not the revelation of the name of God, but the deliverance from Egypt.

God reveals himself in his present/absent being to the individual Moses, but a national liberation was necessary to preserve this revelation. The revelations of art are of narrower scope, but they are designed to be intrinsically self-preserving.

The Greeks too lose faith in their kings, but not—at least before Plato—in their artists. Having liberated themselves through the disintegration of the old hierarchical society rather than through an Exodus from it, they retain the old ritual culture and its theology, but stripped of its power. Instead of the Hebrew religious intuition that cannot be communicated esthetically precisely because it liberates the sacred center from the desiring imagination, the Greeks "liberate" the old sacrificial ethic from its sacred basis by appealing directly to this very imagination. Their first great revealer was not a legislator like Moses, but a wandering poet. If Homer is traditionally depicted as blind, it is not because his visions were more intense than those of Moses before the burning bush, but because his gods, less merciful than that of Moses, did not warn him to avert his eyes. The eternal argument between the Greek and the Hebrew wellsprings of Western culture is whether the minimal kernel of humanity is the inaccessibility of the sacred center or the desire of the human periphery. The course of Western history would seem to suggest that before man can afford to let himself be guided by his desire, he should make sure that the center has been fully liberated from its figures.[5]

* * *

The Mosaic revelation is Hebrew religion's point of departure and its most powerful theological moment. Monotheism and the Exodus, the opening of the center and the liberation from archaic hierarchy, are two movements each of which implies the other. Between the resentfully felt need for departure and its realization, the moment of revelatory liberation must intervene.

Here as elsewhere, the strength of a theology is measured by the ethic it supports. Insofar as this ethic is only implicit in the theology and remains dependent on divine power for its explicit promulgation, the theological revelation is incomplete; but were the theological element to disappear altogether, the revelation would have no center. Western religious history moves toward the paradox of atheological revelation. Can there be revelation without God, and if not, how can the non-necessity or "death" of God be revealed? How can the center be made to appear as liberated, open, without being filled by a divine figure to preserve it from the desires of the periphery? Christianity will offer answers to these questions that still provide the basis for the historical continuity of Western society.

A theology includes an ethic, but is not a mere pretext for it. God's election of Israel could be of value to Israel itself only if God is conceived as preexisting it ontologically. It would clearly be inconceivable within the community to affirm in the manner of Durkheim that Israel's God is a mere emanation of its communal solidarity. Durkheim's interpretation has the undoubted advantage of avoiding the supernatural; but despite its apparent objectivity, by hypostatizing the community of believers into a monadic entity, it forecloses the central question of what constituted this community in the first place. Theology can only be wholly superseded by scientific discourse if the totality of its anthropological content can be absorbed. The theistic position, which positive anthropology has made no attempt to answer, affirms the impossibility of this absorption, in theory as well as in practice. That the source of theological revelation transcends any real and even conceivable human community guarantees to it an intuitive opening of the center that even the most radical and resolute anthropology can never be certain of equalling.

The Mosaic revelation prepares the liberation of Israel that is the founding event of the Hebrew religion and its Judeo-Christian and Moslem descendants. Yet the Exodus does not exhaust the ethical significance of this revelation. The God who reveals himself in the *ehyeh asher ehyeh* offers a defense against resentment more universal than the commandments of the Exodus. The center that reveals itself as hidden, that names itself as a tautological sentence, re-establishes the fundamental equality of every human being before the scene of representation that had been compromised by the founding of hierarchical society. It is only in this perspective of universal liberation, independent in principle of the particular liberation of Israel, that the Mosaic revelation is a definitive theological conquest. But this conquest leads at the same time beyond theology. In insisting only on this supreme moment, we place ourselves at the limit where theology and anthropology become one. It is surely their greater proximity to this limit that explains the disproportionate role of the Jews—that is, of those heirs of Israel who did not accept the trinitary reconstruction of the theological center—in the elaboration of the great anthropological and ideological systems that have given our century its character.

Although the Mosaic revelation is the foundation of the great religions of the West, it was not in itself sufficient to found a universal religion. The Hebrew God is the God of the Exodus. The figure of the Exodus is valuable for all, but only the Hebrews lived it as a people, chosen or more precisely extracted from the old hierarchical world. Christianity and Islam were reactions to a later stage of ethical organization dominated by empires no longer archaic but, to borrow a term from Voegelin, "ecumenical," uniting diverse peoples and cultures under a common administrative hierarchy.

Christianity appears within the Roman world as the bearer of a revelation that addresses each person individually. Mohammed's revelation is again of a collective nature, but it is no longer addressed to a minority, but to the vast and open collectivity of the excluded. Now that Marxism constitutes a "world" in the style of the Christian West, the force of Islam in the "third world," the world of the taken-for-granted, is fully predictable. The command of Mohammed's first vision, "Recite!" is an exhortation to absorb the contents of Judeo-Christian doctrine for the purpose of imparting it to those hitherto excluded from it. As the Christians had already discovered with respect to the Old Testament, to repeat the substance of the doctrine made of the very act of repetition a new, achronological origin. But what the Christians had already done would have to be done still more radically: the Koran's "recital" of the material of the Bible is a full-fledged super-session. Moslem theology is identical in its essence to that of the Mosaic revelation but for its insistence that the monotheistic liberation of the center be made accessible to all through the continuity of this recital.

NOTES

1. *Moses* (Oxford: East and West Library, 1946), p. 55.

2. "God of your father" is parallel to the expression "God of my father" used by Jacob in a few passages in Genesis. Although it is always possible to speculate that the story of Moses' adoption by Pharaoh's daughter is a sign of Egyptian parentage, the text of Exodus refers to Moses' mother Jochebed as a member of the tribe of Levi. Certainly this passage implies no contrast between "the God of your father" and "the God of your mother" or "of your parents"; such expressions are foreign to the Bible.

3. This same experience of the presence of the self before the absolute Other is described by Emmanuel Levinas, implicitly referring to the Mosaic revelation: "The attribute... of the relation to the Infinite is that it is not an unveiling. When, in the presence of another, I say 'Here I am!' this 'Here I am!' is the place whereby the Infinite enters into language, but without letting itself be seen. It does not appear, since it is not thematized, in any case not originally. The 'invisible God' is not to be understood as God invisible to his worshippers, but as God non-thematizable in thought, and nevertheless as not indifferent to the thought which is not a thematization, and probably not even an intentionality" (*Ethique et infini,* Fayard, 1982, p. 112; my translation). Levinas sets himself the task of reconciling revelation with the phenomenological Subject; it is the Other who becomes the occasion of a revelation that does not *unveil.* The Other is an infinite center, and his/her face, for Levinas the occasion of a wealth of meditations, is precisely the contrary of a "figure" that would block the center in the manner of a primitive or cosmological deity. Levinas imposes on us, here and elsewhere, a duty of absolute presence that we know—and that he himself acknowledges—to be at the limit impossible. The rather unapproachable grandeur of this philosophy lies in the fact that it is precisely a *philosophy* whose experiential foundation prevents any recourse to an anthropological hypothesis. For generative anthropology, the "Here I am!" is not given for all time; it could only have become required of us as a result of the opening accomplished by earlier revelations. Certainly, such a revelation was "always already" possible, but its *real* possibility has nevertheless a history. Before Moses, without speaking of all that has happened since, such a "Here I am!" could not have been formulated. And for Moses, there could have been no conceivable identification between the face of the human Other and the unseeable countenance of the

invisible God. It would indeed have been impossible to conceive of the experience of the Other in Levinas's terms before the birth of Christianity.

4.   Thus we have both "John, it's you!" (ostensive) and "John, come here!" (imperative).

5.   This historical lesson can be given a clear economic point; only after its reformulation as a Christian society, that is, as one recognizing the Mosaic revelation, was the West able to develop a modern exchange-system based on the *market*. This is the simplest answer to the familiar crux of ancient history: the failure of classical civilization to evolve into modern market-society. For the market is indeed based on the free circulation of desire, which only the preparatory liberation of the sacred center made possible.

4
The Christian Revelation

CHRISTIANITY IS, like Judaism, a product of revelation; but we would seek in vain in the New Testament a decisive, founding encounter like that of Moses with the burning bush. For the Gospels, Jesus is himself the revealed truth, not a mere witness of it. It is not unreasonable to suppose that Jesus himself had revelatory experiences; but it is significant they have not been transmitted in a recognizable form.[1] Christian theology does not preserve the simple Otherness of its Mosaic origins. Where the Jews worship a non-figural God, Christianity restores figurality to the sacred center. But the figure is not that of a superhuman master; it is that of a human victim. It is the crucifixion that defines the centrality of Christ in the Christian revelation.

The exact doctrine of Jesus, or even his social role—itinerant preacher or "zealot" militant—can only be conjectured. Early Christianity, as we find it in its oldest documents, the epistles of Paul, shows little interest in Jesus' preaching or worldly career. In Paul's writings, Jesus plays for mankind the exclusive role of the Christ, the salvation-bearing mediator whose forthcoming return will bring about the end of man's earthly history. In contrast, the Jesus of the Gospels is above all the prophet of a radically reciprocal morality. The difference between Paul's vision of Jesus and that of the Gospels points to the fundamental theological mystery of Christianity that would later be articulated in the Trinity, a mystery on which the originary hypothesis allows us to shed new light.

* * *

The small group of Jesus's original disciples that had dispersed at the death of its leader did not die out; on the contrary, it regrouped and gained new adherents. The account of the Pentecost in Acts 2.1-41 describes the kind of experience that led to these early conversions:

Acts 2

> ¹When Pentecost day came round, they had all met in one room, ²when suddenly they heard what sounded like a powerful wind from heaven, the noise of which filled the entire house in which they were sitting; ³and something appeared to them that seemed like tongues of fire; these separated and came to rest on the head of each of them. ⁴They were all filled with the Holy Spirit, and began to speak foreign languages as the Spirit gave them the gift of speech.
> ⁵Now there were devout men living in Jerusalem from every nation under heaven, ⁶and at this sound they all assembled, each one bewildered to hear these men speaking his own language.

But scoffers doubt the authenticity of the speaking in tongues, and Peter rises to explain its significance. Peter's address contains the following passage:

> ²²Men of Israel, listen to what I am going to say: Jesus the Nazarene was a man commended to you by God by the miracles and portents and signs that God worked through him when he was among you, as you all know. ²³This man, who was put into your power by the deliberate intention and foreknowledge of God, you took and had crucified by men outside the Law. You killed him, but God raised him to life...

This surprising accusation brought against an audience of potential converts gives a no doubt authentic illustration of the spirit of the early preaching. The resurrection, as confirmed by the glossolalic enthusiasm of the disciples, demonstrates the error of the Jews of

Jerusalem, at the very least passive accomplices in the death of Jesus. This technique relies on the crowd's acquaintance with Jesus and on their feelings of remorse over his death in the face of the affirmation of his resurrection by the faithful. In Peter's discourse, these two key elements— complicity in the persecution of Jesus and the vision of his resurrection—remain entirely separate. It is the crowd who is accused of the murder; the revelations to the apostles as described in the scene of the Ascension at the beginning of Acts (1.6-11) contain no trace of any such accusation. Yet all four versions of the Gospel narrative emphasize Jesus' solitude in his last moments, as well as his denial by this very same Peter who is now so willing to cast the blame on others.

Neither Peter nor any of the original disciples are able to grasp that these two apparently dichotomous attitudes, faith in the resurrected Christ and persecution of the crucified Jesus, here unproblematically opposed and attributed to different sets of persons, are in fact inseparable. Faith and persecution are one: to know Jesus is to have participated in the crucifixion. This insight, inaccessible to those who followed Jesus during his lifetime, is nonetheless the founding intuition of Christianity as we know it, the source of the post-Mosaic theology that would transform a Jewish sect into a universal religion, and that would lead three centuries later to the definitive formulation of the trinitary credo.

Peter's sermon makes the vision of the resurrected Christ appear as the reward of untroubled faith. But there is another text of Acts that shows this vision to be directly linked to, indeed, to be the product of persecution. This text recounts the last biblical appearance of Christ, his revelation to Saul/Paul on the road to Damascus. That this narrative appears three times in the book of Acts demonstrates its exceptional importance. The Epistle to the Galatians (1.11-17) authenticates the experience, if not its precise form. But as in the case of other narratives of revelation, the text is essentially self-confirming.

Acts 9

> ¹Meanwhile Saul was still breathing threats to slaughter the Lord's disciples. He had gone to the high priest ²and asked for letters addressed to the synagogues in Damascus, that would authorize him to arrest and take to Jerusalem any followers of the Way, men or women, that he could find. ³Suddenly, while he was travelling to Damascus and just before he reached the city, there came a light from heaven all round him. ⁴He fell to the ground, and then he heard a voice saying, "Saul, Saul, why are you persecuting me?" ⁵"Who are you, Lord *(kyrie)?*" he asked, and the voice answered, "I am Jesus, and you are persecuting me. ⁶Get up now and go into the city, and you will be told what you have to do." ⁷The men travelling with Saul stood there speechless, for though they heard the voice they could see no one. ⁸Saul got up from the ground, but even with his eyes wide open he could see nothing at all, and they had to lead him into Damascus by the hand. ⁹For three days he was without his sight, and took neither food nor drink.

This first and simplest version of the revelation contains no doubt the authentic kernel of what would later be elaborated in the speeches of 22.3-11 and 26.4-18. The scene takes place only a few years after the crucifixion; Saul is a Pharisee and a persecutor of the Christians. He hears the voice of Jesus asking why he persecutes him; it is this experience that converts Saul to Christianity.

Paul's conversion, the last in the long series of revelations of the resurrected Christ that he himself will modestly summarize in I Corinthians 15, marks the end of the revelatory period of Christianity, and of Western civilization as a whole. Although it is recognized as a great moment of Christian history, its theological importance has been less appreciated. Yet it is the sole revelatory experience of the New Testament that is both historically verifiable and the bearer of a theological intuition of comparable weight to that of Moses on Mount Horeb. The standard commentaries explain Saul's persecution of Jesus as little more than a figure of speech, a metonymy of the persecution that he was exercising against the Christians.[2] But the experience is far more specific. The truth that Saul understands, the power of which is figured in the text by his blinding, is that it is the persecution of the person Jesus that guarantees his presence beyond death and thus demonstrates his divinity. Saul intuits a fundamental connection between persecution and divinization. That the text fails to elaborate this connection, or that Paul's own writings explore it only indirectly, should hardly surprise us. The text of Exodus does not elaborate on the *ehyeh asher ehyeh*. The high point of a revelation is expressed in words that bear the mark of authority precisely because they cannot be explained. In such moments the language of the human subject confronts him as the vehicle of an originary intuition that he would be unable to formulate in conceptual terms.

This text must be read in the light of the Mosaic revelation, which is the model for all biblical revelation scenes. The light in the sky is a sign of divine illumination that has by this time become conventional and no longer requires the natural etiology of the burning bush. This formalization of experience is not a mark of unauthenticity; it reflects a generalization of the revelatory experience that is a product of the prophetic tradition. A more immediate reference is the Ascension recounted at the opening of Acts (1.9-11), which makes the sky the abode of Jesus. The celestiality of the sacred is more clearly marked in the New Testament than in the Old, reflecting the otherworldliness of Jesus' kingdom. The physical occasion of the revelation becomes both more abstract and more subjective: the sky that lights up for a single individual is not much more than a metaphor of a purely internal illumination. Revelation has become, in the etymological sense of the term, an apocalyptic phenomenon. Moses, seeking a solution to the Hebrews' plight, was reminded of their religious unity by the punctual, ritual centrality of the burning bush. Saul, engaged in defending the ritual center against the Christians, learns from the blinding light the vanity of any such attempt at closure.

The structure of Saul's revelation differs most profoundly from that of Moses in the degree to which its content emerges from within. Moses was confronted by an Other to whom he was utterly subordinate and who revealed to him truths about his own being as an ancillary feature of the assignment of his political mission. The theological liberation of monotheism coincided with the political liberation of the Hebrews. What appears to Saul is only his own obsession writ large. Jesus tells him nothing; he only asks a question. For Jesus' identity is itself the revelation, and the mission to which Saul is assigned follows from it.

Both Saul and Moses learn something new about the being who speaks to them; but Saul's is a more radical surprise: the divine voice he hears is at the same time of human origin. Saul first addresses the voice with the term "Lord" *(kyrios)* normally used to address God. Nothing indicates to him that this voice is not that of the God of the Hebrews. Its answer to his question, that it is Jesus who speaks, should not be read as contradicting Saul's original assumption, but as enriching it. God is he who speaks in revelation; if Jesus speaks in this fashion, then he is God. Here as in Exodus, dialogue is the essential form of revelation. What Saul first hears is the accusation of persecution. For him it can only be the God of Moses who speaks, even if he expresses himself in a new fashion; Saul is only open to the word of his own God. His question "Who are you?" expresses the same interrogation of the divine being as Moses' asking the name of God. Great revelations are not emanations of an immutable divinity; they involve a modification of its very substance. Saul, the persecutor of Christians, has just understood that in this persecution he persecuted God. But he can no longer recognize his God; he must ask his identity. It is then that he learns that he is Jesus.

Moses seeks to liberate his people from the Egyptian yoke, but the relationship between this liberation and monotheistic religion is not immediately evident; its necessity appears only *post factum*. Saul, in contrast, is defined for others, and no doubt defines himself, as a persecutor of the Christians; this activity has become so to speak his profession. No doubt the conversion of an antagonistic fervor into the contrary passion is a familiar theme; *odi et amo,* as Ovid put it. Saul's experience is indeed on the borderline of what we would call today an "insight" into his own feelings. But it has not yet crossed this borderline because the persecutorial preoccupation with expelling the hated Other is a source not of personal enlightenment but of theological revelation: he who appears to me against my will is not a mere object of personal obsession, erotic or otherwise: he is my God.

Jesus had appeared to many others before Saul; Saul was the last. What this suggests is that it was Saul who finally understood the point of these appearances where the others had failed to do so. When Jesus appeared earlier, his resurrection was presented as a reward for the faithful. But at his death there had been no faithful; Jesus had been abandoned by Peter and all the disciples. Not that this prevented Peter, as we have just seen, for blaming his master's death on everyone but himself. Saul, in contrast with Peter, had never claimed to be a disciple of Jesus. Thus he alone was able to understand the sense of the resurrection, in a way that allows the non-believer too to understand it and to be converted by it. Jesus returns not to those who loved him, but to those who hated him. Their persecution led him to be crucified, but his return nullifies the effect of the crucifixion and relieves them of their guilt. These are the first manifestations of Jesus' role as divine savior, a role that Paul will be the first to recognize. That the physical manifestations of the resurrected Christ as described in the Gospels or in Acts do not carry the essential message is made clear from Saul's experience. He sees nothing, touches nothing. Jesus' presence to him is attested only through the divine voice, which is, here as in Exodus, the means of communication with the originary scene.

Saul had persecuted the Christians, even participating, according to Acts 7-8, in the lapidation of St. Stephen. Those whom he victimized believed in one who had preached the transcendence of the ethical Law by moral intuition in the awaiting of an imminent apocalypse. Saul, as a good Pharisee, revered the Law, for it alone guaranteed the survival of the Jewish community. But the Law no longer performed the eminently ethical function it had had in the books of Moses. Phariseeism adapted the Mosaic precepts to modern conditions by means of a vast proliferation of secondary rules. The purpose of these rules was less to regulate social interaction than to reinforce by an unending series of symbolic and commemoratory acts the individual's membership in the Jewish community; but the politico-economic functionality of this community in the new world of "ecumenical" empires had become increasingly dubious. In contrast, to espouse the moral intuition expressed in the Sermon on the Mount was to "fulfill" the Law through a radical prolongation of prophetic moralism, to abandon the ethical order of Judaism for an apocalyptic hope in the Kingdom of God.

But the foundation of Christianity as we know it was Paul's intuition that Jesus himself, in the role of the crucified savior, must occupy the central position in the new theology that would guarantee this moral doctrine. Paul ignores Jesus' teachings, but it should not be forgotten that the Gospels that expound them are all the work of followers of Paul. The familiar "humanistic" reading of the Gospels for their doctrine of brotherly love abstracts from the crueler truth of the crucifixion that Paul's deeper anthropological intuition recognizes as fundamental.

Morality and Ethics

The old, pre-Mosaic theologies were born clothed in the ethical systems for which they provided the framework. The Mosaic revelation is revolutionary in clearly detaching its theology from its ethics, but the corollary distinction between ethics and morality remains as yet only implicit. The monotheistic liberation of the center requires the rejection of a hierarchical ontology, but not that of a hierarchical reality. The affirmation of the equality of all men before God is not in itself a moral doctrine. Even the outline of a Mosaic morality that appears in Deuteronomy is never given priority over Moses' ethical legislation. Only in the prophetic opposition to the monarchy will the notion of moral obligation acquire an increasingly explicit independence from ethical law.

Hillel's aphorism that the "golden rule" of morality was "all the Law and the Prophets" reversed the Mosaic priority of ethics over morality, but Jesus alone carried this reversal to its ultimate conclusion. Jewish scholars have often remarked that there is nothing in Jesus' doctrine of moral reciprocity that is not already present in rabbinical reflection. This should not surprise us. It is ethics that are complex and diverse; morality is one. Marxism claims egalitarian morality for its own as the ethic of the proletariat, but it remains the same morality as ever. If that of Jesus and that of Hillel are more or less the same, this is simply because there is no other. The difference lies in Jesus' more radical attachment to his moral intuition.

Morality is nothing but the doctrine of absolute reciprocity in human relations. This exclusive insistence on reciprocity opposes morality to concrete ethics, which are necessarily based on differences. Morality as such has no history; but its formulation as a universal model of behavior independently of any particular ethic is a revolutionary historical event. The rabbis wanted to make morality the heart of their ethic; Jesus understood the liberating force of its constitution as an autonomous ethical model.

The common origin of morality and ethics is the originary scene of representation. The equality of all men before representation is the original foundation of both their equality and their difference in society. Ethics institutes the norms of communal interaction; its revelatory origin is the origin of an order. In the beginning, this order substituted at a crucial moment for the preexistent animal order the mechanisms of which had proven inadequate to their task. But there is nothing in the nature of human order as such that implies equality. The equalitarian foundation of humanity gives no proof of the superiority of primitive equality over the hierarchies that would replace it; on the contrary, this equality belongs to a phase in which the resources of the scene of representation had only begun to be explored. The emergence of "big-men" of various kinds would later show that the real center can be occupied by a man without disturbing the sacred centrality of the scene of representation. But not even the most rigid hierarchy could ever attempt to suppress the fundamental equality of all men before language. The deification of monarchs is nowhere total; the human scene of representation imposes on hierarchical inequality an implicit moral constraint.

The Mosaic revelation gave Judaic moral reflection a theological foundation the absence of which would always be felt in the Greek philosophers' attempts to constitute an ideal ethic, either on the level of the polis or on that of personal relations. Mosaic theology is the living reminder of the absolute difference between the center and the periphery of the originary scene of representation, a difference that provides the foundation of moral reciprocity among men.

The higher stages of moral reflection are concerned with the extraction of the kernel of reciprocity from the concrete ethical precepts that enclose it. The Decalogue illustrates a stage in this process of separation. The uniqueness and the non-figurality of God are combined with injunctions not to kill, not to covet the goods of one's neighbor. But the link remains abstract; the articulation is lacking. Mosaic theology constructs in the Decalogue a general ethic that certainly reflects a moral intuition, but that does not constitute a doctrine of morality in the strong sense of the term.

An ethic maintains a social order; morality, on the contrary, is indifferent to any such order. Morality is a vision of human relations derived exclusively from the reciprocal exchange of signs on the scene of representation. Whatever the intellectual tools and talent of its formulator, at the basis of every conceptual elaboration of morality is the same intuitive kernel, grasped with more or less intensity and clarity. The moral intuition of the Gospels, and no doubt that of Jesus himself, is more extensively developed than that of Hillel, but the basis of the intuition is the same. The exchange of signs at the moment when designation replaces appropriation in the originary scene provides the model of perfect reciprocity that morality extends to the totality of human relations.

No *a priori* frontier separates the affirmations of morality and those of ethics, both of which derive from the same scene. Both the ethical and the moral are normative, proceeding not from empirical observation, but from an intuition of order. But the place of the two fundamental intuitions with respect to this scene is different. Ethical intuition is directed at human relations at the moment when the sacralization of the center through the sign gives way to the sharing of the central object of the communal feast. If the moral is modeled on the exchange of words, the ethical is based on the exchange of things. Morality takes the originary scene as a self-sufficient model of human interaction, whereas ethics is concerned with its prolongation in the economic life of the society. Signs are infinitely reproducible; things are potentially scarce, and access to them must be regulated.

The transcendental origin of the ethical doctrine of the Exodus only confirms this distinction. Moses announces his legislation as dictated by a divine voice; never will Jesus use this procedure. Because the scene itself cannot suffice as the model for the Mosaic ethic, it can only be the place where this ethic is dictated. The role of God in the Mosaic legislation is ultimately that of an arbitrary figure of authority. The classification of certain animals as impure is not a consequence of the nature of God but of previously existing ritual and socio-economic conditions that he is called upon to guarantee. Ethical intuition does not exclude moral intuition, but it must go beyond it in order to imagine how men should live together in the world.

When morality extrapolates from the scene toward reality, it imposes an order on human relations. But this order is no longer a social order, merely an interpersonal one. The rules of morality are addressed to the individual as a person bearing the scene of representation within himself and who is required to regulate his relationships with others according to the model of equality and reciprocity furnished by that scene. Morality affirms this scene to be the originary essence of man. The rabbinical moralist recognizes this ontological priority, but he allows it to be confined to a corner of the ethical edifice; his wisdom understands the prior necessity that a worldly order be maintained in order that human relations, moral or not, can have a material chance of existing. This wisdom is denied by the "scandal to the Jews, folly to the pagans" that Jesus communicated to his followers.

The Gospels inform us far better about Jesus's morality than about his theology. Gospel theology includes too many posterior accretions, mostly post-Pauline, for us to be able to distinguish the original layer of Jesus's teaching. What is striking is just this absence of any clear testimony to an unforgettable theological innovation. Instead of a theological revelation from which, at first implicitly and then explicitly, a moral doctrine would emerge, here the moral doctrine precedes the theology. Jesus situated himself at the most radical point of the prophetic tradition, as a preacher of a moral apocalypse in which the "Kingdom of God" is exclusively characterized by a new quality of interpersonal relations. This preaching brings nothing explicitly new on the theological plane. But the elimination of God's role as the guarantor of an ethical order breaks down the final barrier between human and divine ethical intuition. The transcendence of the Law is the abolition of the Otherness of God, the assertion of ultimate human responsibility for the maintenance of human order.

The moral utopia of the Gospels is based on perfect equality and reciprocity; there are no superiors and inferiors. In such a world, resentment will be abolished. One would therefore think that to hear Jesus' prophecy of his kingdom would be to put away all resentment in this world. That is certainly the sense of the exhortations in the Sermon on the Mount to turn the other cheek, to walk the extra mile. And yet we know that at the end all who had heard Jesus joined forces with his persecutors. Paul's revelation teaches us to take this abandonment in a radical sense; not as mere indifference or fear of the mob, but as participation in its persecutorial hatred. The message of universal brotherhood and love provokes the most violent form of resentment. Paul's conversion-experience, as well as his contributions to the doctrine of the early church, reflect his tacit understanding that this hatred is the fundamental and indeed inevitable reaction to Jesus' moral teachings. Paul leaves these teachings aside because he realizes that their repetition would only continue to produce the same effect.

A phrase like "the first will be the last" informs us as to the probable experiential link between resentment and the moral vision of the Gospels. The sight of a Jewish society whose great families were forced to grovel before the Roman conquerors must have provided Jesus with the intuition that no worldly hierarchy, however "ethical," can maintain itself uncorrupted. The punctilious piety of the Pharisees that makes of the individual the guardian of communal tradition exemplified the futility of all differential practices. The spectacle of a colonialized Jewish society desperately defending its particularity within the "ecumenical" administrative structure of the Roman empire inspires a vision of a world beyond social difference, ruled by universal reciprocity. In this purely moral vision of human relations, each individual is responsible for keeping the peace in his interactions with his fellows. Because the social center is no longer operative, it is for each individual to become his own center, recognizing at the same time the centrality of the other. This vision is essentially polycentric; it cannot be conceived as emerging in revelatory fashion from a single point. On the contrary, he who makes it the content of his teaching must do all he can to efface even the formal sign of centrality conferred on him by the privilege of discourse. The "good news" must spread from mouth to mouth as quickly as possible; it would not be fitting that he who announces it should present himself as distinguished from his fellows by divine election.

With Jesus's doctrine, in sum, the phenomenon of revelation appears outmoded. In announcing the principles of morality as a self-sufficient ethic, Jesus at the same time assigns to each an identical mission ("love thy neighbor as thyself"). In the imminence of the final apocalypse, the incurably sinful worldly order will become transparent to its opposite, the moral order of the Kingdom, where the differential hierarchy of "first" and "last" will be abolished.

But the beauty of this vision should not blind us to its essentially oppositional nature. The universal fraternity will have its contingent of expelled. Even in this doctrine of reconciliation, as in those of the prophets of old, social resentment justifies a figure of reversal: the mighty "first" will be humbled, the humble "last," exalted. Doubtless, this is not the core of Jesus' message. But its presence in the core text of Gospel morality, the Sermon on the Mount, is no accident. Whether or not Jesus himself was vulnerable to resentment, his prophecy of the moral kingdom of absolute reciprocity was born in resentment against social difference and can only be understood in this light. Promulgated in the real world, it denies the ethical differences of this world and reduces the community of its hearers to an undifferentiated collectivity. In other terms, it reduces them to *precisely the status of the proto-human collectivity in the hypothetical originary event.*

It is at the very least implicit in this radical moral preaching that man must be given a new origin. The undifferentiated state in which it leaves its hearers is a slate wiped clean of attachments to preexistent social distinctions. This is prerequisite to the ideal of the autonomous individual sure enough in his own difference to be able to respect that of his fellows. Each will be a center; there will be no periphery. But for the moment, the undifferentiated periphery is all there is. The central position in this configuration is the point from which the word emerges, that is, Jesus himself. By playing this role, whether willfully or not, Jesus focuses all differential attention on himself, becomes the universal object of desire and resentment. Conceived in opposition to worldly difference, the prophecy of the moral kingdom absorbs all difference into itself; the resentment formerly diffused through the social hierarchy is now concentrated on the person of the prophet, who inevitably becomes its unique victim. He who comes to abolish ethical difference arrogates to himself by that very act an absolute difference. The crucifixion makes the prophet of universal reciprocity the unanimously chosen victim of this difference. But as Saul's conversion will demonstrate, and as the parallel with the originary scene suggests, universal persecution is equivalent to divinization.

Here as in his moral doctrine, Jesus is not an absolute innovator, but the most radical heir of the prophetic tradition. The prophet is always a moralizer, always attracts a following, and presumably is always martyred. The four Gospels are one in affirming that Jesus predicted his execution. It is not inconceivable that he even desired it; martyrdom was a recognized sign of prophetic authenticity. In the Gospel narrative (Matthew 23.29-33), Jesus denounces the "scribes and Pharisees" for their continued participation in a succession of murderous and hypocritical generations: the first generation kills the prophet and the second builds him a sepulchre, while murdering the prophets of its own generation. Jesus' final thrust, "Very well then, finish off the work that your fathers began," is a self-conscious assumption of the prophet's role.

The prophet's posthumous glory "recuperated" his martyrdom, which came to be understood as a demonstration of his fidelity to God's truth in the face of the immediate demands of the social order. But moralistic as it may have been, prophetic teaching was always directed to future ethical goals, as the popular vision of the prophet as predictor suggests. Present society martyrs the prophet, but a future society, having witnessed the truth of his prophecies, will recognize his righteousness; his martyrdom does not find its full sense in itself. In the case of Jesus, however, all ethical compromise with a future worldly order is rejected; his kingdom is not of this world. The only thing that he can conceivably prophesy of the worldly future—one which lends verisimilitude to the Gospel story—is precisely his own martyrdom under the condition of the utter abandonment of his message. The prophet banks on a collective memory that preserves his works and keeps them alive; Jesus left no works and we should conceive him at the moment of his death as altogether forgotten.[3] His activity in itself has no continuing power in the absence of his person; whence the crucial role of the resurrection. But as a result of this personal return, which Saul's conversion allows us to explain, Jesus' martyrdom is *wholly* recuperated; it leads not to mere human reverence but to his recognition as a person of God.

We cannot know whether Jesus predicted for himself such a fate. The apocalyptic hope still so visible in Paul's early Epistles to the Thessalonians (around 50 A.D.) may well be a reflection of Jesus' last thoughts on the subject: in the Kingdom of God, divinization would apply to all without exception, each human being henceforth constituting an absolute part of God. As a preparation for the apocalyptic destruction of the worldly order, Jesus' radicalization of prophetic moralizing was the revelation not merely of a new theology, but of theology's self-abolition. For theology is nothing but deferred anthropology; in the Kingdom, we shall shortly see God, and therefore ourselves, face to face.

The perception of Jesus as God is the paradoxical yet inevitable consequence of the "good news" he preached. In revealing his vision of moral decentralization, Jesus found, no doubt despite himself, the secret of absolute centrality. This paradox does not diminish the significance of his moral doctrine, but it allows us to see its limitations. It is useless and even pernicious to curse the incapacity of men to accede to Jesus' fraternal kingdom, as though the Christian vision constituted the total and definitive anthropological truth. Morality cannot be realized directly in the form of an ethic; it can only be approximated through the operation of the modern exchange-system, that is, of the market.[4] But the historical occasion for the development of this system in the West is dependent on the model of self-centralization furnished by the crucified Christ.

* * *

The first Christians—those before Paul—were Jews who continued to believe in the moral apocalypse announced by Jesus, or, more precisely, who began again to believe in it on the basis of the resurrection. The content of their faith must be deduced less from what we know explicitly about Jesus's doctrine than from the reality of that faith itself. For we know a single historical fact about Jesus: that he was crucified. If his disciples had taken him for the Messiah in the traditional sense of king and liberator, his worldly failure would have sufficed to turn them away from him. The fact that, on the contrary, they began to venerate him as a divine being demonstrates that they must have been sensitive to the "recuperation" that we have just described. All share the blame for the unanimous expulsion of the bringer of the good news. But those, like Peter, who are predisposed by a sense of personal guilt become witnesses of the resurrection. This proof that the crucifixion has not eliminated the bringer of the moral message cleanses them of guilt for their complicity in his murder, while attaching them to his person all the more strongly.

In order for the disciples to continue to live in a world whose values they have rejected, they were obliged to create their own community around the moral doctrine of their master. Although Jesus may have preached pure human fraternity, the Christians practiced an ethic mediated by his word. The promulgation of the moral apocalypse had already put between Jesus and his adherents the Mosaic, legislative distance that Matthew figures in the setting of the Sermon on the Mount. But the moral doctrine could not be "remembered" in itself without the guilty participation in the crucifixion and the cleansing vision of the resurrection. Thus once Jesus was dead, his moral teaching, in becoming the common property of all, became even more exclusively his. The Christian community could only found an ethic of reciprocity on this doctrine by installing Jesus in the center as a universal mediator.

These conclusions are drawn less from the conjectured beliefs of the first Christians than from the simple fact of their existence. Their persistence after their leader's death gave proof that the moral revelation had "taken." And so radically simple is the founding anthropological truth of Christianity that one can deduce its essential traits from this simple definition: a moral revelation that has "taken." The conversion, at the supreme moment, of Jesus' disciples into his persecutors was not a sign of the failure of his revelation; on the contrary, it was a proof of its success. Through the resurrection, this persecution itself would be turned into an agent of the moral revelation. But the "taking" of this revelation only becomes assured of historical permanence with the conversion of Paul, who alone grasped the meaning of Jesus' posthumous success. It was Paul who led early Christianity beyond the mere expectation, mediated by the word of the master, of the imminent moral apocalypse of the "second coming." The resurrected Jesus, even as a person of God, has no more temporal power than the living Jesus. But in accepting the indubitable truth of Jesus' accusation that he was persecuting him, Paul, unlike the others, was forced to recognize that the resurrection was not a reward for faith but the return of a victim of murderous resentment. Paul's theology of grace expresses the fact that however sincere the guilt that prompted the resurrection, it could never *deserve* to be purged by it.

Fidelity to Jesus signified the transcendence of the Law, but because Jesus had never taught its abandonment but only its "fulfillment," his followers did not believe they had to separate this fulfillment from the Law itself. Their liberation was a passage through the Law to morality that did not reject its practices, but filled them with a moral sense that, on the model of Jesus' rejection of divorce, may well have made their observance more rather than less strict. Jesus' moral teaching, directed at the individual in his interactions with others, appeared no more to require the abolition of traditional practices than it required refusal to pay taxes to the Romans. These disciples remained Jews while being Christians, all the while presumably blaming, in the Peter's terms, the "Jews of Jerusalem" for the death of Jesus. They failed to understand that, at the moment of their own participation along with the others in his death, they had lost their identity as Jews and had become undifferentiated men-in-general, and that it was as men-in-general and not as Jews that Jesus' return had saved them.

Paul grasped the essential opposition between the worship of Christ and any traditional ethical practice. In a famous sequence in Romans, Paul describes (7.9-10) how the burden of the Law produces in the individual a sense of dereliction: "Once, when there was no Law, I was alive; but when the commandment came, sin came to life and I died." From this living death, only the mediation of the crucified Christ can save him: "When [Jesus] died, he died, once for all, to sin, so his life now is life with God; and in that way, you too must consider yourselves to be dead to sin but alive for God in Christ Jesus" (Romans 6.10-11).

One might well ask, as Christians have indeed asked throughout the centuries, how the Jews were able to maintain the burden of the Law and refuse Christ's mediation. The fact is that Paul's dialectic contains an unspoken moment. The Jew for whom the burden of the Law is too heavy casts it off in order to follow Jesus' promise of the moral apocalypse; but then he finds himself relegated to the resentful, undifferentiated position of the peripheral observer of the central Jesus: the position of his persecutors. The sense of sinfulness felt by such followers of Jesus would thus reflect rather their guilty sense of complicity in the crucifixion than their incapacity to maintain the Law. It is for them that the resurrection brings "freedom from the slavery of sin." The success of Christianity among the Jews remained limited essentially to those who had formed the circle of which Jesus was the center and who could therefore be touched by a sense of remorse for his death. Among the Gentiles, on the contrary, the message of salvation could operate on the more general, less easily contestable guilt of being a member of the resentful mass of mankind.

If the Law had been a burden too heavy to bear, all the less could the Law be replaced as a practical ethic by the interpersonal morality of Jesus, the rigor of which was to that of the Law as the absolute to the relative. Paul understood that it was not obedience to the precepts of Jesus' teachings, but witnessing of his return after his expulsion that was the source of salvation. Because Jesus the bearer of the moral message could not be expelled, his continued imaginary presence was the sign of sinful humanity's reprieve; man had been spared the absolute cutting-off from his origin—damnation—that would have followed Jesus' definitive expulsion. Man is saved from loss of contact with originary morality not by his feeble attempts to put his moral intuition into practice—"good works"—but by the "grace" that allows him access to this intuition in the first place. No act of loving one's neighbor can fulfill the ideal of perfect reciprocity, but the presence of the resurrected Jesus demonstrates that even the most violent act of hatred only reaffirms this ideal. Grace is the demonstration that the "Satanic" desire to stamp out the moral lesson of the originary scene is powerless and self-defeating. But this demonstration cannot be made as an abstract argument; it requires the life of a person.

The moral revelation decentralizes the scene of representation. Brotherly love defines the relations of men in such a way as to ignore the center, whose power dissolves as desire is turned from it. God plays in this system an essentially proleptic role; the promise of the Kingdom gives men the courage to realize it themselves on earth. This is a revolutionary affirmation of the priority of the anthropological over the theological. The role of "God the Father" is reduced to sustaining the originary promise of human reciprocity. The revelation of the divine center was only necessary to maintain men in relative peace so long as they had not yet learned the "good news" that they could do without it. For in the Kingdom of God, all revelation will already have taken place; God will realize his promise by abolishing his external power over man. God will thus be no more than a memory; but this memory of the promise fulfilled will inhabit all men. For the apocalyptic leap will not eliminate past history; universal fraternity will always recall the divine guarantee without which it could never have been realized.

He who proclaims this doctrine announces the existence of the revelatory center in all men; but at the same time he gives his own name to this center. The paradox of Jesus' promise of universal fraternity is that it can only survive in his person. The guarantee of this promise will be provided not by a God external to man, but by a God who speaks with the voice of the rejected Other within man. The divinization of Christ is the recognition that all revelation originates on an internalized scene of representation where each man experiences both his undifferentiated humanity and the absolute otherness of the sacred center.

Through the mediation of the crucifixion and the resurrection, Jesus' doctrine of the moral Kingdom bears with it all of Christian theology. If this is not immediately apparent, it is because the abstract notion of "morality" dissimulates its anthropological foundation. The ideal of moral reciprocity in the totality of human relations is the *telos* of the history that begins with the symmetry of the originary scene. But the announcement of this *telos* cannot simply be attributed to God revealing himself to man; it must come from a man who has understood the existence within himself of the promise that expressed itself in God. We cannot know to what extent Jesus realized that in his enterprise of putting man in the center, he was acting as the ultimate big-man, usurping for himself once and for all God's central position, making himself the unique target of past, present, and future resentment.

* * *

The subject of Saul's encounter on the road to Damascus was not Jesus the propounder of a radical moral doctrine, but the crucified

Christ whose grace will liberate us from sin. Saul persecuted the Christians; his vision transforms this persecution into a proof of Jesus' divinity. "Why are you persecuting me?" is the very substance of this proof.

Paul's revelation teaches him the real meaning of the resurrection that the original apostles like Peter had never understood: that it is not a bodily but a spiritual experience, that it consists in the hearing of a voice rather than in the touching of wounds, and, above all, that it is the direct consequence of the persecution of Jesus, in which all men without exception were implicated. By assuming the status of the central victim, Jesus forces those who persecute him to centralize him in their imagination, to reproduce the operation of divinization as it occurred in the originary event. Jesus' moral doctrine is a radical return to the reciprocity of the origin; but the realization of this reciprocity among the human participants in the originary event proceeds from the isolated central figure of desire and eventual shared consumption. By announcing the moral apocalypse, Jesus assumes the victimary role of this central figure.

Paul's vision shows him that to combat Jesus' doctrine is to persecute a person, and thereby to resurrect his voice. But this voice can henceforth be recognized as speaking in Paul himself, something that Moses could never have said of his God. Once this last external revelation has taken place, all future revelation will come from within; revelatory experience proper will no longer be necessary. Inspired prophecy will play only a marginal role in the evolution of the Christian Church. The fathers of the church are rabbis, not prophets; they are interpreters of a revelation already accomplished.

"Why are you persecuting me?" is a leading question; it presupposes persecution without affirming it, as in the old routine where one man asks another if he is still beating his wife. Jesus' question does not seek an answer, and it receives none in the text. Saul's confession is indirect, non-thematic; if the admission of guilt had not already been made within himself, the scene would never have taken place. To persecute Jesus is to create the conditions for dialogue with him. To desire to expel him is to insure his presence, and thereby to reveal that in persecuting him one in fact desired this presence. The centrality of the God-person is inexpugnable.

The answer to Saul's question "Who are you, Lord?" is "I am Jesus, and you are persecuting me." God is he whom I refuse, whom I wish to extirpate. With Paul, Jesus is converted definitively into Christ; the persecuted man becomes God, or rather already was God. Jesus preached the abolition of the unique sacred center; but Paul saw that this abolition could only be accomplished in each individual through the mediation of this center, persisting as a grace to man despite his desperate wish to expel it. In Jesus' moral vision, each would be a sacred center for the other; Paul understands that the crucified Christ alone maintains the link between humanity and divine centrality. This theological certitude is the necessary precondition for the elaboration of the moral teaching in the Gospels a generation later. The Christian can only be made to participate vicariously in the moral apocalypse once it has been made clear that responsibility for living up to his commitment to Jesus' moral doctrine, a commitment for which he can never be guaranteed sufficient saintliness, has been removed from his shoulders.

Anthropology of the Trinity

The doctrine of the Trinity, which sums up the original contribution of Christian theology, no longer occupies a major place in the religious consciousness of the faithful. A dogma of the Catholic Church and of the majority of Protestant sects, the hot spot of theological controversies for over a millennium, this elegant construction seems devoid of interest for the man of today, for whom the word "person" has acquired connotations quite different from those of its trinitarian use. To quote a recent American work, "Today the trinitarian doctrine is often attacked as unintelligible both in its formulation and in its traditional presentation, and without relevance for modern man."[5] A prominent German theologian comes to much the same conclusion: "Despite their orthodox confession of the Trinity, Christians are, in their practical life, almost mere 'monotheists.' We must be willing to admit that, should the doctrine of the Trinity have to be dropped as false, the major part of religious literature could well remain virtually unchanged."[6] As for contemporary unbelievers, although they continue to view Gospel morality in a favorable light, trinitarian scholasticism seems to them the clearest proof of the unfalsifiable and consequently irredeemably irrational nature of religious thought.

From the perspective of generative anthropology, the Trinity is a structured explanation of the phenomenon of revelation. Needless to say, as a theological doctrine, it is presented as a deduction from a dogmatically defined history rather than as a free hypothesis. But the Trinity is arguably the most highly articulated originary hypothesis possible within the limits of the theological framework. The fact that its dynamic, historical ("economic") aspects are subordinate to its static, eternal ("immanent") ones is a necessary feature of a doctrine which, whatever its anthropological importance, is the basis for a theory of God rather than a theory of man. Yet for the Church, the Trinity is not a revealed truth, but a construction from revelation. Karl Barth[7] considers the Trinity to be the very structure of the revelation of God-for-man, without however going so far as to conceive the relationship of God to man in the context of an anthropology.

Let us first briefly summarize the doctrine. God is a single substance in three persons: the Father, the Son, and the Holy Spirit. The Son is engendered by the Father, or proceeds from the Father by generation; the Spirit proceeds from the Father and from the Son by "spiration," a *sui generis* term that designates spiritual as opposed to material production. (The Orthodox Church, by rejecting the word *filioque*—"and from the son"—in the Constantinopolitan creed, differs from the Western churches in considering that the Spirit proceeds from the Father *through* the Son. The higher degree of symmetry between father and son in the Western doctrine makes it a more radical and abstract, less "paternalistic" Christianity.) Although the Father is the cause of the two other persons, he precedes them neither in time nor in any ontological order.

The Trinity presents to theologians the challenge of explaining its threefold perfection on the basis of the idea of a single perfect God. From Augustine to Thomas Aquinas, the traditional form of this explanation develops by way of the analogies furnished by human consciousness.[8] The generation of the Son, which is that of the Word or *logos,* proceeds by "similarity"—we would say by *representation.* The "spiration" of the Holy Spirit, on the other hand, proceeds by "difference," such as we experience in willing or loving—we would say, by *desire.* For Barth, the three terms are explained as Father/Revealer, Son/Revelation, and Spirit/Revealedness.[9] The Father, inaccessible to the senses, "generates" the revelation of the Son, producing at the same time the Spirit as the revealedness of the Father in the Son; the analogy of representation/similarity and will/difference is applied here, but in a context essentially determined by the presence of man as the beneficiary of revelation. Barth's is a more "economic" or (human) salvation-oriented version of the Trinity than that of the great Catholic theologians, one which is thereby all the more congenial to our anthropological hypothesis.

Revelation has for its object the structure of the scene of representation, as the originary hypothesis presents it. The unity of the scene is evident; all is concentrated around its central object. But Trinitarian theology suggests that the relationship of man to the center has three inseparable modalities:

(1) The central being is inaccessible and as such possesses a force of repulsion that keeps men at a distance from it, and from each other; it thereby guarantees communal peace. Thus the object is the source of difference, the originary referent of the sign that also appears as its generative force; the sign is produced by the men on the periphery as if at the command of the center.

(2) The central being as object is the collective victim, a gift made to the community by the force inhabiting the central locus and incarnating itself in it; like the Son, it gives its body for the faithful to consume. In this role, the object is the "signified" or idea *(logos)* of the referent made accessible to the human periphery.

(3) The central locus is the revelatory opening produced by the double nature of the being insofar as it is (1) generating (2), the divine power generating its concrete incarnation as coequal with it and inseparable from it, or in linguistic terms, as signifying it. In offering itself as an object of appetitive and intellectual satisfaction, the inaccessible object-of-desire reveals its love of men and to men.

Master, victim, opening are the three modes of existence of the center of the originary scene. These modes constitute for the participants three distinct modalities of the sacred-significant-being. Personhood is implicit in each of the three because the most fundamental definition of a person is that which can be the origin of a word. The originary word designates its referent as both master and victim; but the word is only an act of *parole,* the *logos* as an utterance in history, to the extent that the *langue* that is the ahistorical ground of its meaning inheres in the central being. And the place where the "type" and the "token" necessarily come together is the scene itself. What connects the particular utterance with its general meaning is our experience of the referent-as-signified-by-the-signifier, an experience that is only possible insofar as the scene of representation is at the same time an objectively identifiable communal locus and one possessed by each of us in our internalized scene of representation. The Spirit is given to all human beings as a guarantee of their access to the scene of human language, which is the primary characteristic of their humanity.

The Augustinian triad that comes closest to that implicit in the foregoing discussion is: (Father) object seen, (Son) external vision, (Spirit) attention of mind.[10] The "object seen" is a reality independent of our vision, a "thing in itself." The "external vision" is *our* image of the object, its signified, seen as outside us. And the "attention of mind" that links the objective object/referent to the subjective image/signified is the scene of representation on which the substantive identity of object and vision is understood.

To the extent that we ourselves are persons only thanks to the scene of representation, this attribution of "personhood" to the components of the scene forces us to recognize the place whence we speak. The trinitarian doctrine stands in opposition to metaphysics, which situates the origin of language in the domain of "pure spirit," that is, nowhere. The Spirit is the locus of the word, but it is a *situated* locus.

Every sentence of trinitarian theology can be translated into a proposition concerning the scene of representation; and the theological intuition that is expressed in its best pages is a sure guide for anthropology. The in-existence of the three persons who participate equally in being describes the unity of the scene and the equal necessity of its components. The generation of the Son by the Father through similarity corresponds to the manifestation-as-victim of the inaccessible center. This generation does not create an ontological or temporal priority, for the object is master only inasmuch as it is victim; its mastery is manifested only when it is the object of the desire that will make it an object of communal consumption. The counter-intuitive aspect of a doctrine that refuses temporal priority to the Father over the Son, insisting rather on the fact that fatherhood comes into being simultaneously with the generation of the child, is a demonstration of the anthropological sureness of its founding intuition. The "spiration" of the Spirit by the Father and the Son is their common giving of meaning to the central locus of the revelation, which exists only through the becoming-victim of the master-object, guaranteeing that we can know their substantive equivalence. The Western *filioque* is anthropologically justified by the symmetry of the two first elements in its creation; to say with the Orthodox church that the master-object creates the revelatory opening only "through" the victim-object is to remain bound by the historical priority of sacrificial monotheism, in which the victim is only a *locum tenens* for the deity.[11]

Thus the trinitarian doctrine elaborates in theological language and within the limits of the theological perspective a general theory of the scene of representation as it is constituted in the revelatory event. The trinity is eternal-immanent, but also revelatory-economic, which is equivalent to saying that the structures of the originary scene are at the same time those of the human person who is constituted by it.

In the original hypothetical scene, master, victim, and central locus are distinguished by the different physical behaviors that they provoke in the participants at the periphery. The object-master prevents the act of appropriation, the object-victim is divided and eaten, and the center is designated as the locus of appearance of the master-as-victim by the aborted gesture that has become the first linguistic sign. On the imaginary scene of representation that is constituted within each participant of the originary scene, the components are no longer visible to the naked eye, but their structure of opposition/identity remains the same. The desired object is at once master and victim, victim insofar as it is master and master insofar as it is victim, and the necessity of this conjunction makes possible the revelation of the object as such to our imaginary contemplation. Augustine's insight that the scene of human consciousness has the same structure as the Trinity is an affirmation of the originary structural identity of the internally and the externally realized scenes of representation—of God and man.

The scene of representation retains its "trinitarian" structure throughout all its modalities, whether it be the scene of language, of fiction, or of desire. The center is at once Father/master/inaccessible, Son/victim/assimilable, Spirit/opening/intelligible, and this triplicity is not an arbitrarily extendable series but a closed totality. Every representational event is a revelation; the structure of consciousness is revelatory. The least of these revelations is in principle irreversible, leaving its trace in memory, just as the greatest, those the memory of which is preserved by biblical faith, designate the fundamental stages of our understanding of the scene on which they appear.

* * *

This brief sketch of an interpretation of the trinitarian doctrine as the kernel of a general anthropological theory illustrates how human science can profit from the reflection inspired by religious faith. The transformation of the Christian doctrine of the Trinity into a trinitarian anthropology of the scene of representation does not require the sacrifice of its historicity on the altar of atemporal structuralism. A theory that claimed to reveal the structure of this scene once and for all would deny itself the possibility of understanding its history. What faith preserves are the principal historic stages of the revelation of this structure, and the persons of the Trinity are named with respect to the event that closes the revelatory series, the revelation of Christ as Son/victim. But as human science, generative anthropology posits the historicity even of the "timeless" or "immanent" structure that trinitarian theology makes asymmetrically the source but not the product of the "economic" human history of revelation.

Religious faith opposes the significance of particular events to any universal reasoning from empirical data. It links the atemporal truth of man to the temporal truth of revelation, holding structure and history together for so long as rational thought remains incapable of joining them. The originary hypothesis accomplishes this synthesis without abandoning anything of religious truth but its certitude. For a religious faith that claims itself definitive, generative anthropology substitutes a scientific faith that acknowledges its provisional nature.

What is linked by *re-ligio* is in the first place the human community. Whence the strength of the sociological anthropology of Durkheim, for whom the sacred is the community incarnate. But the fatal weakness of this explanation of the sacred is that the community is not a preexistent entity from which the sacred can be derived; it is founded in the act of linking, which is a communion before a revelation. Religion affirms this communion; its rites celebrate it as an event while its discourses declare it eternal. Faith has for its object the eternal presence of what has been present, and this bond between atemporal presence and historic having-been-present, between the fixed order of the scene and the event of revelation, holds the community together from the first to the last moment of its history.

But as soon as we speak in general terms of "religion" or "faith" we too risk falling into structuralism. The truth that is revealed and preserved as presence is not indefinitely extensible. The end of the revelatory phenomenon in the West corresponds, not to the "end of history" of human truth, but to the isolation of the minimal structure of the scene of representation from the historical constraints of its revelation to man. Henceforth mankind will possess a sufficient self-consciousness to be able to pursue the revelatory dialogue on its own, independently of celestial intervention. Each individual soul is a participant in the Spirit and so to speak an anthropological laboratory open to the lessons of human history. The apparently freer opening that metaphysics claims to provide isolates the scene from its human context and thereby precludes the possibility of thinking it in its origin and in its history as the form of being-for-man.

NOTES

1.   The only experience of Jesus related in the Gospels that might conceivably be called a revelation is the Temptation (Matthew 4, Mark 1, Luke 4), which is the work of "the Spirit." The tempter's failure demonstrates Jesus' invulnerability to what we have called the "negative revelation" of resentment.

2.   See for example E. Haenchen's *The Acts of the Apostles: A Commentary*, 14th ed., English translation, (Oxford: Blackwell, 1971), p. 322: "Whoever persecutes the Christians persecutes Christ."

3.   It is worth noting that the absence of written works attributed to Jesus cannot simply be explained by the presumed "fact" that he never wrote any. The attribution of the writings of the Old Testament prophets is hardly clearer. What is significant is not whether Jesus wrote anything down, but that it never occurred to anyone to attribute any writings to him. Jesus must be forgotten and remembered wholly in the context of dialogue; his encounter with Saul is exemplary of this.

4.   To prove this affirmation would require another book. I can only give the outline of an argument here. The Gospel utopia is founded on the absolute centrality of each individual. But this centrality is based on difference, and in traditional society, social difference means the creation of a small elite at the top of a steep hierarchy. The modern market-system, as exemplified by contemporary "consumer society," is a system that generates ever more elaborate means of differentiating among its members. Although resentment is certainly not abolished, each individual is taught by the market-system to treat all others as equally unique individuals. Imperfect as it is even as an abstract model, highly differentiated consumer society (and not the uniformized utopias of socialism) is the historical realization of the decentralization of the Gospel utopia: the most moral society for the greatest number.

5.   Edmund J. Fortman, *The Triune God: A Historical Study of the Doctrine of the Trinity* (Philadelphia: The Westminster Press, 1972), p. xxvi.

6.   Karl Rahner, *The Trinity*, tr. Joseph Donceel, (New York: Herder and Herder, 1970), p. 10-11. (Originally a part of the collective work *Mysterium Salutis*, vol. 2.)

7.   We refer to his masterwork, *Kirchliche Dogmatik*, 4 vols., (Zurich: EVZ-Verlag, 1957-67); or in English, *Church Dogmatics*, 4 vols., eds. G. M. Bromiley and T. F. Torrance (Edinburgh: T. & T. Clark, 1956-75). The relevant section is I, 2, *Die Offenbarung* (= Revelation).

8.   Augustine's psychological analogies *(vestigia)* of the Trinity are the basis for the understanding of the doctrine in Western theology. He formulated many triads on the Father, Son, Spirit pattern, among which the best known are: mind, knowledge, love; memory, understanding, will. Thomas' *Summa Theologiae* provides the definitive statement of medieval Church doctrine concerning the Trinity. For bibliographical references and further historical information, the reader is particularly referred to Edmund Fortman's *The Triune God* (reference in note 5) and Michael O'Carroll's *Trinitas: A Theological Encyclopedia of the Holy Trinity* (Wilmington: Michael Glazier, Inc., 1987).

9.   Barth's terms are *Offenbarer/Offenbarung/Offenbarkeit*. The middle term could no doubt be just as well translated as "revealed," and the third by "revelation," but the English translation reserves *revelation* for the second term and *revealedness* for the third. Although *revelation* is indeed the normal English translation of *Offenbarung*, it masks the fact that in Barth's usage this word designates rather the thing revealed than the revelatory act. In the trinitarian context, this is surely meant to emphasize the unity of the Father who reveals *himself* in the Son: the act of revelation and the "thing" revealed are one. Thus the Spirit is the Revealedness of the Father as Son.

10.   See *Trinitas*, (reference in note 8), p. 45 for references.

11.   Needless to say, there are points to be made on both sides of this controversy. The Greek position is to begin with the separate persons of the Trinity, starting with the Father, thus following the historical process of the evolution of Christianity from Judaism. The Western position wants to grasp the divine essence simultaneously in the three persons. Eastern religion respects history and gives if not an ontological then a heuristic priority to the Father, whereas the more radical Western position is concerned more with the Trinity as *system*. The latter is closer to scientific anthropology, but it must be said that the former is more sensitive to the question of religious epistemology. The West, as opposed to the East, is more speculative, more willing to envisage the scene as a whole rather than limiting itself to the point of view of the spectators within the scene.

5
Conclusion: Science and Faith

THE BARRIER that separates religious belief from scientific theory seems easy enough to locate, if not to demolish. Science proposes hypothetical models, verifiable in principle; faith presents its founding truths as self-justifying. By agreeing to define the opposition in formal terms and to avoid discussions of content, the believer and the scientist succeed in averting confrontation. Neither side is anxious for dialogue, particularly when both sides coexist in the same individual.

It is not by chance that the only subject over which faith and science still come to blows is that of the origin of man. The creationists or "creation scientists" insist that Genesis be taught to children alongside, or even in place of, the theory of evolution. It is easy to deride those who reject the Darwinian theory out of hand because it "makes man descend from monkeys"; the affirmation that God created man in his own image is not a sufficient foundation for anthropological science. But if the alternative proposed by creationism is insufficient, the question it raises cannot be swept aside with such good scientific conscience. As we saw at the beginning of this work, the theory of biological evolution does not explain the emergence of man. The Bible is a better source of materials for the solution of this problem than the Olduvai Gorge. Human science has done well to purge itself of religious faith, but it is still unable to assimilate the event-linked anthropological truth that faith transmits. This truth is by no means limited, as both creationists and evolutionists seem equally ready to believe, to the narrative of the first chapter of Genesis. The story of the Passion or the moral diatribes of the prophets provide far more precious insights into the evolution of human consciousness than volumes of primitive myths.

The scientists' inability to make use of these texts is easy to understand. The scientific methodology by means of which man has conquered nature and transformed the world abhors dogmatic affirmation. The Bible does not present hypotheses; it affirms revealed truths. But the Bible is an invaluable source of anthropological hypotheses for the human scientist who has understood that man is from the beginning the product of a particular, not a "universal" history. Cultural affirmations, however dogmatic, of the influence of specific revelatory events on this history are not mere artifacts for ethnological classification; their conceptual content is of direct anthropological interest.

The believers, for their part, have been equally unable to translate their offended intuition into a dialogue with science. The militant defenders of this intuition have a deficient understanding of the spiritual needs of modernity and no concept whatever of its intellectual needs. In contrast with the militant sects, the great churches have learned to make their peace with human science, but without ever perceiving the contribution that the revealed truths they cherish could make to it.

Faith is generally opposed to reason on a naively phenomenological level in terms equally unfair to both. "Faith" and "reason," construed as the religious attitude and the scientific attitude, are dubious abstractions. If faith can be reduced to an attitude, then the mythology of an Amazonian tribe is as valid as the theology of Thomas Aquinas. Indeed, it is more so, for the latter attempted to formalize the structures of his belief, whereas his primitive counterpart has the good taste to leave this task to the ethnologist. Only by taking into account the *content* of faith can one begin to conceive its synthesis with scientific thought. But to do this would require us to take seriously the content of our own Judeo-Christian tradition, something that only the least sophisticated still have the ethnocentric bad form to do.

Conclusion: Science and Faith

The theological endpoint of this tradition, the doctrine of the Trinity, has provided us with a model closely homologous to that of our anthropological hypothesis. Skeptics might call this a suspiciously easy triumph. On the one hand, our theory may be modeled, unconsciously or by design, on Judeo-Christian theology; on the other, the "anthropological" notions we find in religious texts have little in common with the meanings that believers traditionally attribute to them.

The Western religious tradition has been marked more than any other by the liberation of the scene of representation from ritual constraints and by the assertion of human mastery over it. The ancient Greeks were perhaps the first people to display systematic intellectual curiosity, but the scientific method is a product of Western Christian civilization, with its roots in medieval nominalism.[1] The association of modern science with the Christian West cannot be explained away. Nor does the fact that the early scientists were opposed by the Church constitute a counter-demonstration.

Yet the relationship between biblical theology and natural science is relatively distant and a considerable intellectual effort is required to mediate between the two. The claim of this book is both stronger and more easily demonstrable: not merely does the theological liberation provided by the Judeo-Christian tradition facilitate the development of scientific thought, but the contents of this tradition are themselves contributions to scientific thought.

Natural science is a consequence of intellectual liberation, but it does not concern itself with this liberation. In contrast, human science cannot ignore the conditions of its own origin, because self-understanding is an essential characteristic of man. I would go farther and assert that it is *the* essential characteristic of man. Language emerged in order to re-present the conditions of its own emergence. Ritual and myth are models of man's origin. Even the most primitive culture is "theoretical," not because of some mysterious human drive to "disinterested contemplation," but because man's survival depends on his ability to reproduce the communal peace of the originary event.

The primary purpose of man's language and other systems of representation is to maintain and reinforce the order that this event instituted among creatures who could no longer operate under the conditions of animal societies. "Know thyself" is man's categorical imperative.

Religion can most simply be defined as the activity that commemorates human origin. Animals have communication-systems, but they have no religion because they have no originary event to commemorate. Once we are able to recognize that religion is the essential pre-scientific form of practical anthropological knowledge, then it becomes altogether reasonable that the religious foundation of the most highly developed and successful social system should contain a reservoir of material of value to anthropologists. The interest of this material appears all the greater when one observes positive anthropology's failure not merely to solve but even to formulate the essential questions relevant either to defining man's difference from his fellow primates or to constructing a theoretical model of his emergence. Just as the lowly Hebrews and not their Egyptian masters developed the first modern religious system, so it may well be the role of scientific "amateurs" to develop the first generative anthropology. As in many other examples of the "law of unequal development," the inhabitants of the margins have the advantage of observing a wider field than those fixed in the center of things.

In defending our use of biblical material there is a temptation we must avoid. The little word "metaphor" lends a facile respectability to religious and even superstitious practices. But the weakening of homologies to metaphors clears the ground of controversy so well that it leaves no residue by which one could decide the false from the true. The apologists for "metaphoric" religion would have us believe that religion consists of some excellent moral beliefs with a gratuitous supernatural element thrown in. They reassure us that the latter is no real obstacle, because we can admire the moral doctrine while understanding the supernatural as "metaphorical." Yet it is not the attachment to supernatural beings but to *historical particularity* that differentiates religious faith from scientific hypothesis. The supernatural is a system of reinforcement, the *credo quia absurdum* that encourages the believer to repulse the temptations of a simple-minded rationalism. It is very fine to seek to understand the world with one's unaided reason, but the latter is by no means guaranteed to bring one closer to the truth than dogmatic acceptance of the faith of one's ancestors. The supernatural serves as a guard-rail for the person who risks losing his faith in the historically specific for lack of logical justification.

We have all experienced the sort of argument, most frequently political, in which our adversary gains a dialectical triumph without changing any of our convictions. As we return to our home base to sharpen our polemic swords, we rely on reassuring figures that allow us to feel in the right, on what today are called, a little too easily, "myths." Religion, whose basis in experience is farther from daily life than politics, surrounds the revelation that is its object of faith with such protective myths. These may be "demythologized" without difficulty into metaphors, but this procedure will not lead us to the historical object of faith. On the contrary, the reduction of the dogma of faith to a plethora of metaphors and symbols puts us at a great risk of defining not a religious experience but a *literary* one. By dint of humanizing Christianity, one obtains a "humanitarian" Jesus who makes a fine romantic hero but who is incapable of bearing either the historical weight or the anthropological truth of the Christian experience. The process of demythologization gets caught up in the details and forgets about preserving the sense of the whole. A structure like the Trinity, so rich in anthropological insights, can be purged of its mythical components only once these insights have been recognized and absorbed.

Even the most subtle dialectic cannot assimilate the believer's existential intuition of divine presence to a hypothesis of human science. But that is not my aim; and this "believer" is perhaps more difficult to find today than one might think. Even the toughest faith will be worn down through contact with science unless it makes the effort to understand that it has nothing to lose in this contact but its resistance to the free examination of its truths. These truths are real, and faith does not have to sacrifice them to science; on the contrary, it should insist that science take them into account. For the truth of man is at once eternal and historic, and a science too ensnared in metaphysics to recognize this proves to be less of a science than faith itself.

NOTES

1.　See Hans Blumenberg, *The Legitimacy of the Modern Age,* tr. Robert M. Wallace (Cambridge, Mass: MIT Press, 1983) for a discussion of the medieval roots of Renaissance science.

Bibliography

Barth, Karl. *Kirchliche Dogmatik*, 4 vols. Zurich: EVZ-Verlag, 1957-67. English translation, *Church Dogmatics*, 4 vols., eds. G.M. Bromiley and T. F. Torrance. Edinburgh: T. & T. Clark, 1956-75.

Blumenberg, Hans. *The Legitimacy of the Modern Age*, tr. Robert M. Wallace. Cambridge, Mass: MIT Press, 1983.

Buber, Martin. *Moses*. Oxford: East and West Library, 1946.

Derrida, Jacques. *De la grammatologie*. Paris: Minuit, 1968.

Durkheim, Emile. *Les Formes élémentaires de la vie religieuse*, 4th ed., Paris: PUF, 1960.

Fortman, Edmund J. *The Triune God: A Historical Study of the Doctrine of the Trinity*. Philadelphia: The Westminster Press, 1972.

Freud, Sigmund. *Moses and Monotheism*. New York: Vintage, 1958.

——. *Totem and taboo : some points of agreement between the mental lives of savages and neurotics*, tr. James Strachey. London: Routledge & Paul, 1961.

Gans, Eric. *The End of Culture*. Berkeley: University of California Press, 1985.

——. *The Origin of Language*. Berkeley: University of California Press, 1981.

Girard, René. *Des choses cachées depuis la fondation du monde*. Paris: Grasset, 1978.

——. *La violence et le sacré*. Paris: Grasset, 1972.

Haenchen, E. *The Acts of the Apostles: A Commentary*, 14th ed., English translation. Oxford: Blackwell, 1971.

Levinas, Emmanuel. *Ethique et infini*. Paris: Fayard, 1982.

Nietzsche, Friedrich. *On the Genealogy of Morals*, tr. Walter Kaufmann. New York: Vintage, 1967.

———. *The Will to Power*, tr. Walter Kaufmann and R. J. Hollingdale. New York: Vintage, 1968.

O'Carroll, Michael. *Trinitas: A Theological Encyclopedia of the Holy Trinity*. Wilmington: Michael Glazier, Inc., 1987.

Popper, Karl. *The Logic of Scientific Discovery*. London: Hutchinson, 1979.

Rahner, Karl. *The Trinity*, tr. Joseph Donceel. New York: Herder and Herder, 1970.

Rousseau, Jean-Jacques. *Discours sur l'origine et les fondements de l'inégalité parmi les hommes*. Cambridge: Cambridge University Press, 1947.

Sahlins, Marshall. *Stone Age Economics*. Chicago: Aldine-Atherton, 1972.

Scheler, Max. *Vom Umsturz der Werte*. Leipzig: Der Neue Geist, 1919.

Voegelin, Eric. *Order and History*, 4 vols. Baton Rouge: Louisiana State University Press, 1956-74.

Index

Abraham, 11, 50, 57, 76
Achilles, 43
Acts of the Apostles, 86-91
Agamemnon, 43
Akhenaton, 47, 52
anthropology, generative, vii, 2, 19, 22, 108, 113, 120
anthropology, positive, 1-2, 8, 80
apocalypse, 101, 106-107
Aquinas, Thomas, 109, 116, 118
arbitrariness of signifier, 4, 27-28
Arunta, 30, 34, 46
Ascension, 87, 89
Augustine, 109-110, 112, 116
autoprobatory, 50-51, 58, 77, 87

Barth, Karl, 108-109, 116
Bataille, Georges, 34
behaviorism, 21
Bible, 11-13, 50-84, 117-118
big-man, 33-39, 41, 43-46, 59, 94
Buber, Martin, 51-52, 60-61, 70-72

Camus, Albert, 44
Christianity, 42-43, 49, 80-82, 85-116, 121
community, virtual, 16, 28
I Corinthians, 88
Creation Epic, Babylonian, 37, 40
creation science, vii, 117
crucifixion, 85, 91-92, 99, 101, 105, 107

Damascus, 87-88, 105
Darwin, Charles, 6, 117
death of God, 38, 80
Decalogue, 94
declarative sentence, 32, 63, 73
deconstruction, 10, 67
deferral, 14, 18-19, 39
Derrida, Jacques, 18
Deuteronomy, 93
dominance, 4-5, 25, 29, 36
Duhm, 70, 72
Durkheim, Emile, 30, 80, 113

Egypt, 37, 46-47, 49-53, 56-59, 65-66, 74-75, 78, 120
election, 38, 80
Engels, Friedrich, 11
equality, 25, 29-31, 41-42, 47, 59, 66, 78, 93-94
ethics, 65, 92-104
ethnocentrism, 18, 41, 118
ethnology, 10-11, 30
exchange, 37, 39-40
Exodus, 49-84, 89-90, 95

faith, 1, 6, 12, 21, 25, 87, 113-114, 117-118, 121-122
Feuerbach, Ludwig, 11
Foucault, Michel, 22
Frazer, James, 12
Freud, Sigmund, 11, 52

Index

Galatians, 87
Genesis, 117
gesture, aborted, 4-5, 23-24
Gospels, 85, 91-92, 96-100, 107, 115
grace, 102, 104, 107
Greeks, 31, 36-37, 78-79, 119

Hebrews, 31, 36-37, 43, 47, 49-84, 89-90, 120
henotheism, 47
hierarchy, 29-33, 36, 40-42, 44-46, 57, 73, 79, 81, 93-94
Hillel, 93, 95
Homer, 34, 79

imperative, 32, 63
individualization, 46-47
Isaiah, 65
Islam, 49, 80-82

Jerusalem, 86-87, 103
Jesus Christ, 12, 85-107, 113, 115, 121
Jews, 85-86, 97, 103
Judaism, 31, 36, 42, 49-85, 94, 116
Judeo-Christian tradition, 11, 13, 23, 60, 80-81, 118-119

Kant, Immanuel, 25
Kingdom of God, 92, 96, 98, 100, 104-105
Koran, 82

Law, Jewish, 92-93, 102-104
Levinas, Emmanuel, 83-84
Lévi-Strauss, Claude, 11, 30
linguistic maturity, 63

Mallarmé, Stéphane, 15
market, 84, 100, 115
Marx, Karl, 11, 52
Marxism, 13, 49, 93
Matthew, 99, 101
Messiah, 101

minimality, 3, 5
modernity, 31, 118
Mohammed, 81
monotheism, 31, 62, 68, 79, 90, 92, 111
morality, 92-105, 107
Moses, 11, 42, 50-85, 88-90, 92, 94-95
Mowinckel, 70, 72
myth, 7-11, 37, 40, 67, 119, 121

New Testament, 88-89
Nietzsche, Friedrich, 42, 67

Oedipus, 66
Old Testament, 89
oral law, 61
originary hypothesis, vii, 1, 7, 9, 14, 23, 26, 41, 49, 51, 68, 85, 108, 113
Orthodox Church, 108, 111
ostensive, 5, 62-63, 71, 73, 84
Otto, Rudolph, 70
Ovid, 91

Passover, 77-78
Paul/Saul, 85, 87-92, 97, 100-107, 115
Pavlov, Ivan, 3
Pentecost, 86
persecution, 87, 89, 106-107
Peter, 86-87, 91, 101, 106
Pharaoh, 52, 66, 74, 77
Pharisees, 92, 99
Plato, 79
Popper, Karl, 18
positivism, 7-13, 21, 39
potlatch, 33
primitive culture, 30-32, 36, 41
prophetic tradition, 99

redistribution, 34-35, 37
resentment, 42-46, 62, 81, 96-99, 105
resurrection, 87-88, 91, 101-103, 105-106

INDEX

revelation, secondary, 32, 35
rhetoric, 67
ritual, 12, 16-17, 34-35, 39, 54, 89, 119
Rome, 81, 97, 103
Rousseau, Jean-Jacques, 31-32, 36
Rumi, Jelaluddin, 70-71

sacrifice, 34, 54
Sahlins, Marshall, 33
Saussure, Ferdinand de, 18
scene of origin, 2-3, 5-7, 14-16, 19, 24, 34, 45, 49, 57, 93, 98, 100, 112, 119
scene of representation, 23, 26, 28, 35-36, 41, 47, 63, 105, 112, 119
Scheler, Max, 44
Sermon on the Mount, 92, 96-98, 101
Sisyphus, 44

Smith, Robertson, 12, 30
Sophists, 22
speciation, 6
spiration, 108, 111
Stephen, Saint, 91
structuralism, 30, 113-114

Thebes, 35, 66
Thessalonians, 100
Trinity, 81, 85, 87, 107-113, 115-116, 119, 121
Tylor, Edward, 12

universality, cultural, 32, 41

Veblen, Thorstein, 34
Voegelin, Eric, 19, 81

YHVH, 61-62, 64, 69-77

ABOUT THE AUTHOR

Eric Gans was born in New York City in 1941. He attended Columbia University (B.A. 1960) and received his doctorate in Romance Languages from the Johns Hopkins University in 1966. Mr. Gans's principal field of specialization is nineteenth-century French literature. He is currently professor of French at the University of California, Los Angeles, where he has taught since 1969.

Mr. Gans's previous works *The Origin of Language* (1981) and *The End of Culture* (1985) develop the theory of Generative Anthropology, founded on the hypothesis that human language, and therefore man himself, originated in a unique event. He is currently working on a new synthesis, tentatively entitled *Principles of Generative Anthropology*. His recreational activities include computer hacking and distance running.